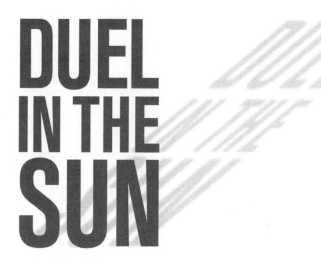

DUEL
IN THE
SUN

DUEL
IN THE
SUN

ALBERTO SALAZAR, DICK BEARDSLEY,
AND AMERICA'S GREATEST MARATHON

JOHN BRANT

RODALE

© 2006 by John Brant

Printed in the United States of America
Rodale Inc. makes every effort to use acid-free ∞, recycled paper ♻.

Excerpts on pages 5, 14, 40, 78, 104, and 109 from *Staying the Course*
© 2002 by Dick Beardsley and Maureen Anderson with permission.

Book design by Christopher Rhoads

Library of Congress Cataloging-in-Publication Data

Brant, John, date.
    Duel in the sun : Alberto Salazar, Dick Beardsley, and America's greatest marathon / John Brant.
        p.   cm.
    Includes index.
    ISBN-13 978–1–59486–262–5 hardcover
    ISBN-10 1–59486–262–1 hardcover
    1. Salazar, Alberto, 1958–   2. Beardsley, Dick.   3. Runners (Sports)—United States—Biography.   4. Boston Marathon.
    I. Title.
    GV1061.14B73   2006
    796.42'52092—dc22   2005030917

Distributed to the trade by Holtzbrinck Publishers

2   4   3   6   8   10   9   7   5   3   1   hardcover

For PG

ACKNOWLEDGMENTS

The gracious cooperation of Dick Beardsley and Alberto Salazar has made this book possible. The Beardsley and Salazar families also provided invaluable guidance; special thanks to Jose Salazar. Bill Squires, who coached the two runners, generously and memorably coached me through my re-creation of their 1982 Boston Marathon.

David Willey, editor-in-chief of *Runner's World,* encouraged me to pursue this story, shaped and guided it through each stage of the magazine editorial process, and gave it room to fly. Thanks also to Amby Burfoot, Adam Bean, Charlie Butler, and the editorial staff at *Runner's World.*

Hal Higdon and Tom Derderian each have written excellent histories of the Boston Marathon, and I am indebted to both authors. Maureen Anderson expertly assisted Dick Beardsley in his fine autobiography, which was also a key source. Thanks to Kirk Pfrangle, Jack Fleming, Carole Ross, David Hobler, Bruce Leonard, John Lodwick, and Paul Raether for their insights and recollections. Don Kardong gave me a boost when I needed it, and Bob Wischnia, who has saved me from looking like a fool many times, did it again while I was writing this book.

Thanks to Joe Henderson, Dave Kuehls, Laura Hohnhold, Marty Post, Jim Harmon, John Lehrer, and the late George Sheehan. Special thanks to Dan Ferrara for his faith in the word and true-north friendship.

The estimable Lisa Considine and Leah Flickinger, my editors at

Rodale, filled my sails throughout the voyage, and Sloan Harris, my agent, guided me through all weathers. Thanks also to Jeremy Katz and Zach Schisgal for their editorial judgment and to Christopher Rhoads for his artful book design.

My family members far and near, especially my parents, Fern and Ray Brant, have served as steady beacons. Thanks to Steve Brant, David Jensen, Paul Gribbon, Fred Leonhardt, and to my comrades in the Oregon rain.

Above all, my love and gratitude go to Patricia Gregorio and our children, Tom and Mary. They inspire every good sentence I have written.

PROLOGUE

In front of some audiences, Dick Beardsley never even mentions the 1982 Boston Marathon. In fact, he barely touches upon his running career at all. When he's delivering one of his regular talks to a 12-step group, for instance, he simply begins, "Hi, I'm Dick, and I'm a drug addict," then launches into the heartrending story of his disease and recovery.

When Beardsley finishes speaking and the people are wiping away their tears and settling back into their seats after a standing ovation, the host might explain how Dick Beardsley is the fourth-fastest American marathoner of all time and that his race with Alberto Salazar at Boston in '82 remains one of the signature moments in the history of distance running—perhaps in the history of any sport.

But other audiences, such as this one at the 2003 Royal Victoria Marathon in Victoria, British Columbia, know all about Beardsley's athletic career and are eager—even hungry—to relive his legendary "duel in the sun" with Salazar.

There's a considerable amount of preamble first. Beardsley is not good at leaving things out. Appearing the day before the race at an expo accompanying the marathon, he tells the crowd of 200 about getting creamed at his first high school football practice, quitting the team, and turning out for cross-country without knowing quite what it was. "Do they tackle you in cross-country?" he asked a friend.

He recounts the time he had to rouse a college professor out of bed so the professor could administer a makeup exam that would preserve Beardsley's undergraduate athletic eligibility and tells how he snuck into a sporting goods show disguised as a sales rep in order to beg his first shoe sponsorship deal. He explains that he ran his second marathon in a brand-new pair of running shoes that he didn't want to get dirty by breaking in and that he prepared by fasting for 4 days because he'd read somewhere that fasting worked in ultramarathons, so he figured . . .

Beardsley is blessed with the fundamental trait of a born entertainer: a complete lack of self-consciousness. He strides back and forth in front of the podium, laughing right along with the audience, as delighted as they are by his own buffoonery. His voice—honking, booming, unabashed—rolls around the conference hall in overpowering waves. Wearing jeans, a red pullover, and a blue fleece vest, whipcord lean and with a lilt to his step, Beardsley might be mistaken for an athlete in his prime rather than a man of 48. You have to sit close to notice the hard miles showing around his eyes.

The crowd's laughter drowns out the canned rock music blaring from the expo midway next door. But when Beardsley shifts gears, traveling back to Hopkinton, Massachusetts, on that sunny afternoon of April 19, 1982, the room falls raptly silent.

This only seems appropriate because the 1982 Boston Marathon was great theater: two American runners, one a renowned champion and the other a gutsy underdog, going at each other for just under 2 hours and 9 minutes. Other famous marathons have featured narrow margins of victory, but their suspense developed late in the race, the product of a rapidly fading leader or a furiously closing challenger. At the '82 Boston, by contrast, Beardsley and Salazar ran in each other's pockets the entire 26.2 miles, with no other competitor near them for the final 9 miles. They were so close that, for most of the last half of the race, Beardsley, while in the lead, monitored Salazar's progress by watching his shadow on the asphalt.

Neither man broke; and neither, in any meaningful sense, lost. The race merely came to a thrilling, shattering end, leaving both runners, in separate and ultimately Pyrrhic ways, the winner. The drama unfolded in the sport's most storied venue, at the peak of the first running boom—when the United States produced world-class marathoners in the profusion that Kenya and Ethiopia do today and when thousands of passionate citizen-runners embraced the sport as a means of personal and cultural transformation.

The next day's headlines read, "An Epic Duel," "The Greatest Boston Marathon," and "A Display of Single-Minded Determination and Indefatigable Spirit." Since Beardsley was just 26 and Salazar 23, everyone assumed that this would be the start of a long and glorious rivalry, one that would galvanize the public and seal American dominance in the sport through the 1984 Olympics and beyond.

But rather than a beginning, Boston '82 represented a climax. After that day, neither man ran as well again. Since that day, the sport of distance running has grown in numbers, with a half million Americans completing a marathon in 2003. But it has lost much of its rigorous, ascetic glamour. One hundred thirty-five runners, for instance, virtually every one an American, ran the '82 Boston in a time of 2 hours 30 minutes or faster, the benchmark for a first-rate marathon. In 2003, only 12 runners, 3 of which were Americans, met this standard. Since that day, incredibly, only two more of the world's major marathons have been won by a native-bred American man. So some of the younger members of the audience—the elite runners who will lead tomorrow's Royal Victoria Marathon—listen to Beardsley's story with a mixture of curiosity, envy, and awe.

Others in the crowd, those closer to Beardsley's age, listen on a different frequency. They know the enormous toll that Boston exacted on both Alberto Salazar and Dick Beardsley. If the glory of their marathon bore a heroic quality, so did their suffering and deliverance afterward.

⬡

At Nike corporate headquarters in Beaverton, Oregon, Alberto Salazar descends to the ground floor café of the Mia Hamm Building for a quick lunch (another office building on campus is named after Salazar, but he has made it a point never to work there). For the past several years, Nike has employed Salazar, the most recent great American distance runner, as a kind of coach-at-large, chartered to deliver the long-awaited next great one. On this drizzly October Tuesday, he has spent the morning training the professional athletes in Nike's ambitious Oregon Project. This afternoon, he'll supervise the cross-country team at Portland's Central Catholic High School.

Both teams, he reports, are thriving. The Oregon Project's Dan Browne has met the qualifying standard for the 2004 Olympic marathon trials, and Central Catholic's Galen Rupp—a gifted young runner for whom many predict greatness—is preparing to repeat as the state cross-country champion. Other parts of Salazar's life are in similar bloom. His oldest son, Antonio, plays wide receiver for the University of Oregon's football team; and his younger son, Alejandro, is a star striker for the University of Portland's soccer team.

At 45, Salazar appears every bit the proud, happy family man and flourishing professional. His brown eyes are clear, calm, and bright; and his cheeks have lost a marathoner's hollowness. He no longer resembles "the young priest fresh from seminary whose face drives all the housewives to distraction," as one writer described him 20 years ago. Now Salazar looks more like a fit-but-comfortable middle-aged monsignor, a man still true to his religious vocation, but also at ease in the worldly realm of fund-raisers and cocktail parties.

A Japanese visitor approaches and politely asks for an autograph. Salazar graciously complies. "After Boston, I was never quite the same," he says after his fan has departed. "I had a few good races, but everything became difficult. Workouts that I used to fly through became an ordeal. And eventually, of course, I got so sick that I wondered if I'd ever get well."

Salazar's warm smile briefly turns wintry. For a moment, his poise falters, and he seems like a traumatized man who, after long therapy, can finally talk about his past.

"It took me a long time to connect the dots," he says, "and see that the line stretched all the way back to Boston."

1

Monday, April 19, Patriots' Day, broke warm and blue over Boston, perfect for just about anything except running 26.2 miles. At a little after 7:00 a.m., Dick Beardsley stood at the window of his room at the downtown Sheraton, watching work crews ready the marathon's finish-line area on Hereford Street far below. Behind him in the room, his wife, Mary, slept. He was glad to have her with him, but it also felt somewhat strange. Normally, when Beardsley traveled to road races, Mary stayed home in Rush City, Minnesota, where she worked as a secretary in an insurance office. But Mary had wanted to see the sights in Boston and support her husband at the crucial moment of his career.

Although it had lost some of its luster in recent years, the Boston Marathon remained the world's most famous distance run, defining the sport for the general public the way Johnstown defined floods. Americans became horse racing fans on Kentucky Derby day and auto racing fans on Memorial Day for the Indianapolis 500; on Patriots' Day (commemorating the battles of Lexington and Concord and the start of the Revolutionary War), they turned their brief attention spans to the Boston Marathon. Even Beardsley's father in Minnesota knew about the race. When Dick had started running as a high school junior, his father had given him a special birthday present—an IOU plane ticket good one day for a trip to the Boston Marathon.

A decade later, Dick had finally made it to Boston for the marathon's 86th running. His father, however, hadn't paid a cent for the trip; the only thing Bill Beardsley was interested in buying was his next fifth of gin. Nor did the race organizers offer appearance or prize money (those emoluments wouldn't come to the race for a few more years). New Balance, Beardsley's shoe sponsor, was picking up his tab.

Tradition and prestige, not cash, had drawn Dick to Boston. Most big-city marathons, for instance, started early on Sunday morning. Boston, by contrast, always started at noon on Monday. Instead of getting out of bed and proceeding directly to the starting line, as was his custom, Dick now had 5 long hours to fill. He wasn't hungry, but he knew he needed nourishment. He tiptoed to the phone and ordered toast and hot chocolate from room service.

As he nibbled the toast and sipped the cocoa, he watched the *Today* show, turning the volume down low so as not to disturb Mary. Willard Scott, the weatherman, predicted bright sunshine and a high of 75 degrees for the Boston area. "A great day for the marathon," he said.

"Shows how much you know about the marathon, Willard," Beardsley murmured to the screen.

Dick flicked off the TV and moved back to the window. His edginess transcended normal prerace jitters. He felt as if he were standing at a precipice, as if something momentous lay in store. By predilection and economic necessity, Beardsley liked to race nearly every weekend. Combined with his $25,000 annual stipend from New Balance, prize winnings from 10-Ks, marathons, and other road races earned him and Mary the semblance of a middle-class income. For the last 3 months, however, Beardsley had forgone the road-race paydays, sequestering himself in Atlanta, where he trained exclusively—and furiously—for Boston. Two weeks earlier, he had logged his last hard workout, 20 miles at 2-hour, 12-minute marathon pace over a hilly course. Later that day, he'd reported the results to his Boston-based coach, Bill Squires.

"I couldn't feel my feet touching the ground," Beardsley said. "I felt like I was flying."

"You damn fool!" Squires screamed into the phone. "You just left your marathon in Georgia!"

But Beardsley knew he had plenty left in him. During training, he typically ran 120 to 140 miles per week, an average of just under 20 miles a day. In the 2 weeks before a marathon, when he cut that mileage to 70, he felt like he was barely running at all. He couldn't sleep. The energy boiled out of him.

He pushed aside the cup of chalky hot chocolate and took a long drink of cold water. The only defense against the heat was to drink all morning, flush his tissues with water, and keep drinking all through the race. Maybe Salazar wouldn't be so careful.

For a while, Dick sat in the chair, his feet up on the table, by turns watching the TV and the morning light rising on Hereford Street. He sipped water, made frequent trips to the bathroom, and, as he'd been doing continuously for the last month, thought about Alberto Salazar. On Thursday night, Dick had watched on the TV news as Salazar arrived at Logan Airport.

"There's no other runner here who especially concerns me," Salazar had told the reporters. "If de Castella or Seko were competing, it would be different. But looking at the rest of the field . . . let's just say I'm fit and prepared. If there are no injuries or unforeseen developments . . . well, the facts are plain; I'm the fastest man in the race."

There was no disputing Salazar's facts: He was clearly the

fastest man in the race. For the last few years, he had been the fastest man in just about any distance race on earth. Salazar owned the world record in the marathon—2:08:13. He was the two-time defending champion of the New York City Marathon. On the track, he was the second-fastest American ever in the 10,000 meters and a member of the 1980 Olympic team. He'd been an NCAA cross-country champion and last month, in Morocco, had finished second in the world cross-country championships. The state of Salazar's present fitness was daunting; just 9 days earlier, he'd run 27:30 for 10,000 meters, 2 seconds off the American record and almost 2 minutes faster than Beardsley's best for that distance. Salazar, moreover, was handsome and charismatic, the closest the sport of running came to a household name. After his world-record performance in New York City last autumn, *Sports Illustrated* published a long, adulatory profile of him. President Ronald Reagan congratulated Salazar at a ceremony at the White House.

Beardsley had run against him once before, at the 1980 New York City Marathon, Salazar's debut at the distance. Then a 22-year-old senior at the University of Oregon, Salazar had swaggered into the media capital of the world and publicly announced that he would run the race faster than 2:10, the standard for a world-class marathon. At the time, Beardsley's personal best for the distance was 2:12. All through race week, he watched Salazar cut around Manhattan in a black leather jacket, looking like a young Montgomery Clift.

"Alberto wasn't exactly bragging; he was just extremely confident," Beardsley recalled. "He had already trained with Bill Rodgers, who was the reigning champion of the marathon, and he knew that he was in just as good of shape as Billy—in fact, a lot better shape. He didn't predict victory, just that, if the day went reasonably well, this is how he would perform. It's not really bragging if you back it up."

On the day of the marathon, Beardsley broke fast from the start on the Verrazano Narrows Bridge and by midrace had established a significant lead over the rest of the pack. He held the lead through the 18-mile mark, which came at the Manhattan end of the Queensboro Bridge. When Beardsley swooped down from the bridge, which was closed to spectators, the roar from the crowd lining First Avenue nearly staggered him. Bill Squires, who had recently begun coaching Beardsley, stood among the crowd. He was shocked to see his runner so soon. "Holy shit, Dickie!" he screamed. "You're leading the New York City Marathon!"

It seemed too good to be true, and it was. Just beyond the bridge, Salazar blasted past Beardsley without a glance, gliding on to a commanding 2:09:41 victory. Salazar had logged the fastest debut marathon ever and delivered the time that he'd promised. Beardsley, meanwhile, faded to a ninth-place, 2:13:55 finish. As close as he'd come to Salazar, however (at the finish, roughly two-thirds of a mile separated them), he might as well have been 90th.

So what would be different here in Boston 18 months later? Everything, Dick vowed. "My whole life boiled down to this," Beardsley would remember in his autobiography. "One way or another, this race would change everything. . . . I was a runaway train. That's how it felt. My times were getting so much better so much faster, I had no idea where it would lead."

He sat down again at the TV and, by reflex, started drumming his thighs with his fists. All through the winter, as he sat in front of the TV in the evenings, Dick pounded his thighs 1,500 times. He had read somewhere that pounding your muscles made them tougher. If he thought it might gain him a few seconds on the downhills, he would have tried curing his quadriceps in a smokehouse.

Beardsley knew that the Boston Marathon would be decided on the course's four long hills rising between miles 17 and 21. If he had any chance of beating Salazar, he would have to fly down those hills like a bobsled racer, capitalizing on the fact that Salazar outweighed him by 20 pounds. Conceivably, a series of rocketing descents might pummel Salazar's legs to the extent that Dick would be able to pull away from him before mile 25. If that plan failed, and the race came down to a kick at the end, then Salazar, with his superior short-range speed, would do the pummeling.

Mary stirred and sighed in bed, mumbling a few words from a dream. Dick couldn't make out what she said. He stared, unseeing, at the TV. Fifteen hundred punches, each thigh.

At 9:00 a.m., he kissed Mary, who wished him good luck and said she would see him at the finish line; she planned to watch the race on TV in the hotel room. He gathered his gear and went down to the lobby to catch his ride out to the start in Hopkinton, a village of 2,500 people 26 miles west of Boston. To transport its sponsored runners, New Balance had organized a station wagon—a green behemoth with three rows of seats, the first two facing the front and the third facing the rear. The rear bench-seat was the kind little kids rode in, goofing around, wrestling, tormenting the drivers of trailing cars with endless waves or, if they were nasty kids, obscene gestures.

To Dick's dismay, all the front seats had been taken up by other runners and their gear. They were good marathoners, 2:15 to 2:20 caliber, but none would contend in today's race. Beardsley, by contrast, had won the inaugural London Marathon the previous spring and last June had achieved a breakthrough 2:09:36 victory at Grandma's Marathon in Duluth, Minnesota. Until Salazar's entry into Boston a month earlier, Beardsley was considered a favorite to win the race. Moreover, he was New Balance's top athlete; in fact, just last night, a representative from Adidas had made a strong pitch—including an offer of a $25,000 signing bonus—to try to lure Beardsley to his company. Out of loyalty, Dick had refused. This was his reward? Why couldn't those guys make room for him in the front? Maybe he should have signed Adidas's contract after all.

Dick jammed his gear bag into the cramped rear seat, then squeezed in beside it. He was isolated from the other athletes, facing away from them, like a naughty, exiled 9-year-old. Often he felt like a 9-year-old. Weighing all of 128 pounds, he wasn't much bigger than one. His dad was a drunk in Wayzata, Minnesota, and so was his mom. His college? South Dakota State University. He hadn't graduated. He lived in a rented log cabin by the St. Croix River in eastern Minnesota, an hour's drive north of the Twin Cities. The only places he felt truly at home were the woods and dairy barns and the gravel roads through farm country where he could run for hours with no company but the cows, nothing to look at but the mile markers. Beardsley sulked in the far back seat. The rear window was stuck open. He shivered from the cold air rushing in and felt nauseous from the exhaust fumes.

All winter he had suffered these mood swings—moments of supreme self-confidence, when he would feel as invincible as Salazar, followed by moments of crushing doubt, when he knew he was an imposter, that he really wasn't a world-class athlete, that at some critical point God would expose him as a sad little son of small-town alcoholics. Dick was just a dairy farmer, for crying out loud. He did not belong in the front of the station wagon, and he certainly didn't belong in the front of the Boston Marathon. He be-longed on a Minnesota lake trolling for bass and crappies or in a dairy barn, sitting on a three-legged stool, staring into the yin dark-ness of a Holstein milk cow, her tail flicking flop. He belonged in the rear seat of a funky old station wagon, looking backward like a 9-year-old.

The station wagon moved out of the Back Bay, heading west through the bright morning sunshine, passing Kenmore Square bars already filling up with Patriots' Day revelers. His father would start drinking in the morning, too. Bill Beardsley loved martinis. He kept an inch or two of gin in his glass all day long.

For the duration of the drive to Hopkinton, the station wagon's rear window was stuck open. Exhaust fumes wafted in on a chilly wind. Dick shivered and gagged; but just as his discomfort cli-maxed, he was able to dissociate, jump outside of himself for a mo-ment. What a comical sight he must make, he thought, shoehorned into the back of a giant old station wagon. Dick gave a thin smile. He repositioned his bag, fashioning a pillowlike perch away from the draft. It really wasn't so bad back here, he thought. At least he didn't have to talk to anybody.

As the station wagon cleared the city and turned west onto the Interstate 495 expressway, Beardsley's gloom and anxiety gave way to confidence. One other thing was true: He felt at home in the marathon.

2

Had the founding fathers of Hopkinton magically descended on their town on the morning of April 19, 1982, they would have been dumbfounded by the marathoners' presence, yet at the same time comforted by it. Early Hopkinton was a resoundingly Puritan place, hacked out of the Massachusetts wilderness in the late 1600s and officially founded in 1715. King Philip of the Wampanoag Indian tribe waged desperate, bloody war against the colonists, who responded in kind, slaughtering the natives with impunity. For its first few centuries, the history of the town was the same as that of the Hopkinton Congregational Church. The church and town were chartered to spread the Puritan gospel— specifically, to support Harvard College in its mission to produce ministers of that gospel. The church was led by heroic clergymen such as Nathaniel Howe, who presaged the endurance feats of latter-day marathoners by preaching his entire career without a raise in salary (the church elders felt that earthly rewards had a corrupting influence on pastors), supplementing his meager stipend by plowing fields, mucking stalls, and bucking hay. The Reverend Howe, perhaps, would have felt a special kinship with the thousands of citizen-runners massed in the town square that sunny morning.

There were 6,689 entrants, one of the largest Boston Marathon fields up to that point. As recently as 1968, the field for the race had been less than 1,000. Indeed, for most of the Boston Marathon's 8 previous decades, only 100 or so male marathoners showed up each Patriots' Day (no woman attempted to participate until 1966, when 22-year-old Roberta Gibb stepped out of the bushes near the starting line and ran the race unsanctioned). Prior to the 1960s, the marathoners were mostly New England workingmen. Seven-time champion Clarence DeMar, for example, labored in a local print shop. Three-time winner Johnny Kelley, who ran the marathon into his nineties, was a maintenance man for the Boston Edison Electric Company. "I think the job toughened me up, climbing and walking and stooping all day," Kelley said. "When I began my run at night, I was tired; but after a mile or so, the tiredness went away."

Hopkinton understood and welcomed such men. If Patriots' Day was cold or rainy, village residents opened their homes to them. As soon as the runners left the town square, Hopkinton, with its white church and green square and World War I doughboy statue, returned to its quiet rhythm. If they had the day off from work, residents washed their cars or took down their storm windows or walked down to the doughnut shop to rag with their neighbors about the Red Sox's chances that year, whether Ted Williams still had the snap in his wrists.

Then came the running boom. By 1969, the marathon's field swelled to more than 1,000. Instead of a few dozen pipe fitters, warehousemen, and out-of-town eccentrics, the village was invaded by hundreds of mostly long-haired baby boomers. Attorneys from Tampa and clinical psychologists from Santa Cruz now peed behind the rhododendrons. More marathoners showed up every year, fusing the new running ethic to the Boston Marathon's venerable traditions. Along with most other aspects of the race, Hopkinton adjusted. The start, however, was no longer a charming, small-town production. Now it was portable bathrooms and popcorn vendors. A fleet of buses ferried the runners from Boston, dumping them out at Hopkinton High School to guzzle Gatorade and slather their thighs and toes with Vaseline to ward off the day's chafing. The atmosphere now resembled that of a rock festival or an outdoor religious revival.

The Boston Marathon would have been a much bigger circus if its organizers, the Boston Athletic Association, had still taken all comers. Starting in 1970, however, marathoners had to meet a standard to gain entrance: A man younger than 40 had to run a certified marathon in 2:50 or better, a man 40 or older in 3:10 or better. For women, the respective standards were 3:20 and 3:30. By setting the bar so high, organizers hoped to limit the fields to 1,000, but they underestimated Boston's appeal and the depth and commitment of the running nation. In 1979, for example, near the apex of the first running boom, a total of 7,877 entrants met Boston's near Draconian requirements. This was remarkable. In order to run that fast, a citizen-runner had to train virtually as long and hard as a professional athlete.

Indeed, the zeal of Boston's rank-and-file marathoners rivaled, and in some ways echoed, the religious passion of Nathaniel Howe and his congregation. The runners indulged in orgies of self-denial—running 100 miles a week, working junk jobs in order to have time to train, paying their own way to races, banding together in ascetic cells, forgoing the temptations of an idolatrous world in order to attain grace and salvation out on the road. As in Puritan New England, grace was not blithely attained. A believer—a runner—earned it by losing toenails and training down to bone and muscle, just as the Puritans formed calluses on their knees from praying. No one made a cent from their strenuous efforts. The running life, like the spiritual life, was its own reward.

So in April 1982, the village of Hopkinton was still built upon a church, and each runner milling in the town square that morning was a kind of priest. The proof of their election lay in the very fact that they were present; they had met Boston's forbidding standard. And the highest priests, the most blessed and immaculately chosen, were the elite runners, who, befitting their status, were afforded a private refuge—in the basement of the First Congregational Church, of course—to gather themselves for the ordeal ahead. When the station wagon full of New Balance runners barreled into Hopkinton and emptied its passengers, however, the lone high priest among them unfolded slowly from his cramped berth, then turned away from the church.

Beardsley was supposed to meet Bill Squires here at 10:00 a.m., but it was almost 10:30 before the coach emerged from the crowded town square. "Christ, Dickie, there you are," said Squires as if Beardsley, and not Squires, was the one who was late. "C'mon, let's get outta here." He made a dismissive gesture toward the church, where, inside, Alberto Salazar prepared to run. "You don't wanna go breathing those other guys' gas."

Squires hooked Dick's arm and led him away. The coach, as usual, was a sight. He wore a rayon Day-Glo-bright sweater, with plaid golf pants and a shiny blue pair of New Balance 710 running shoes. A Bear Bryant–style tweed fedora held down his toupee, which, thank goodness, seemed to be plastered on tightly today. At the Falmouth Road Race a year ago, a gust of wind had blown the hairpiece sideways on the coach's head. Squires didn't realize his predicament, however, and Dick and the other runners didn't have the heart to tell him. They kept straight faces until Squires had departed, then howled with laughter.

"I found us a place where you can relax, have a little privacy," Squires said. "This little old lady on Taylor Street, just the next block over."

But the street wasn't the next block over, and it wasn't two blocks over. In fact, Hopkinton didn't have a Taylor Street at all. When the coach asked a cop where Taylor Street was, he got a blank stare for an answer. Squires waved his hand and charged on ahead. All Dick could do was follow. It was a typical Squires production. Ask him a simple question and he'd launch into a 20-minute-long discursive fugue, which might include raunchy jokes, scraps of show tunes, and tall tales about guys running stakes races at county fairs in Vermont in the 1890s. But just as you were completely tuning him out, Squires would come around to answering your question, and the reply would always be dead-on. By the same token, there was a purpose behind this seeming wild goose chase. Squires knew Dick had been obsessing about Salazar. In the final hour before the competition, he wanted to keep Beardsley as removed from the race excitement as possible.

Beardsley and Squires had been collaborating for a year and a half, during which Dick had progressed from a journeyman professional distance runner to a world-class marathoner. They had met in August 1980 at the Falmouth Road Race on Cape Cod. "I'm sitting in a coffee shop and this kid comes in all starry-eyed," Squires remembered. "Nice farm kid. Sincere, but not frightened. Some of these kids come to you, they look like guppies. You wanna say, 'Come on, kid, go buy some roller skates, get lost.' But Dickie wasn't like that. You could tell that underneath all that aw-shucks crap he was tough as nails.

"We start talking workouts, and he wants to show me his training log. I said, 'Jesus Christ, I don't wanna read that thing. The only thing I read is the obituaries in the morning paper to see if I'm still alive.' Dickie laughed at that—this big, booming laugh. I knew then that this kid was all right."

Beardsley, for his part, had been awestruck. Squires was 50 years old at the time and a legend in the American running community. A former star miler at Notre Dame, Squires served on the faculty at Boston State University but had gained fame as the coach of the Greater Boston Track Club, which had incubated the careers of four-time Boston Marathon winner Bill Rodgers and, a few years later, a 16-year-old prodigy named Alberto Salazar.

Squires also served as the coach of the New Balance Track Club, the shoe company that had recently signed Beardsley to an endorsement contract. At the end of that first weekend in Falmouth, the coach offered the runner his services.

"He might as well have told me I was pregnant, that's how much trouble I had believing this was happening," Beardsley remembered in his autobiography. "We were at lunch, and right away he started scribbling some workouts on the backs of napkins. It was the start of a very strange and very exciting long-distance relationship."

Squires was a master of the marathon in general and of the Boston Marathon in particular. He possessed an encyclopedic knowledge of the course and an uncanny ability for helping runners perform at their best on it. He was also a colorful and eccentric personality. Squires seemed to belong to a different time, the Damon Runyan era when, as Beardsley's experience attested, coaches held court in coffee shops and saloons and jotted workouts on the margins of the sports page. Squires's presence invoked images of a winter Saturday night in the city, a track meet on the boards at Boston Garden, corned beef and cabbage on the steam tables, snow on the sidewalk. Yet the coach also got along well with the younger, long-haired crowd and was beginning to reach a wider audience. That afternoon, he would provide color commentary for the Boston Marathon race telecast.

Beardsley and Squires lurched around Hopkinton for a quarter hour before happening across a tidy white clapboard house with black shutters. "Here it is," Squires said, gesturing to the house with a proprietary flourish.

Dick followed Squires into the house and met the nice little old lady who lived there. The coach immediately went into his patter. "How do, missus, beautiful day, lovely home, let me introduce Dickie Beardsley here from Minnesota. Dickie's a dairy farmer, got hay stuck in his teeth, but don't be fooled. In a few minutes, he's gonna run the Boston Marathon, and just between you and me, he's got a shot to win it if he sets his mouth right and does the hubba-hubba on the hills . . . "

The lady led Dick upstairs. She had set aside a bedroom for him, with an adjoining bathroom with fresh towels. "Is there anything else I can get for you?" she asked.

"No, ma'am, this is just great. Gosh, you've knocked yourself out for me. I can't thank you enough."

The lady beamed. Little old ladies were always beaming at Dick Beardsley. "Dick was our sport's best-known 'good guy,'" Bill Rodgers said. "Everyone in the running community liked Dick."

Beardsley would have loved to hang out with the woman and talk about the weather in Hopkinton and the state of her cabbages in the backyard garden. But now wasn't the time. The lady returned downstairs. While she and Squires yakked, Dick stretched out on the bed with his water bottle and tape deck and earphones. The coach had given him a white painter's cap to wear during the race for protection against the sun. Dick sipped water, listened to a Dan Fogelberg tape, punched ventilation holes in the cap with his pocket knife, and thought again about Salazar.

For the last few weeks, since Alberto had committed to run

Boston, Dick had spent practically all his waking moments—and some of his sleeping ones—thinking and dreaming about him. Beardsley's friends commiserated when Salazar's entry became public; now Dick's chances of winning the marathon had been sliced to near zero. But in fact, Dick welcomed Salazar. His presence helped him focus, gave him something tangible to work against. Alberto Salazar became Beardsley's mountain to climb. Meanwhile, as his televised arrival at the Boston airport attested, Salazar seemed to regard Beardsley as beneath his contempt. It was almost like a romantic attraction—the more Alberto ignored him, the more passionately Dick wanted to beat him. Or at the very least make the SOB know he was there.

"Okay, Dickie, I gotta shove off. Call the race for all the ships at sea." Squires was standing in the doorway. Dick pulled off his headphones and started to get up.

"Stay put," Squires said. But Dick stood and shook Squires's hand. They locked eyes briefly, then looked away. Dick broke the awkward silence, giving Squires advice on his TV appearance that afternoon.

"Remember, Coach, you've got to assume that your microphone's always on. Don't go thinking you're hanging out at the Eliot and start telling your stories. I don't want to have to bail you out of jail for violating the decency code."

"Aw hell, with that babe what's-her-name and that guy with the hair, I'll be lucky to get a word in edgewise."

They again fell silent. Dick worried that he would choke up. Squires's crusty exterior was just that; underneath, he was a kind and thoughtful man. During the weekend they had first met, for instance, Beardsley had stayed at a house in Falmouth with the coach and several other runners. Beds and sofas had been scarce. When Squires saw Beardsley trying to sleep sitting up in a chair, the coach ordered him to take his own bed. Later that night, when Dick rose to go to the bathroom, he discovered Squires asleep in the bathtub.

"You got your cap?" Squires said to him now. "You got your sponge?" He went off on a riff about the '78 race, when the temperature was nearly 90 degrees, eventually working around to his final instructions. "Now look, remember, all you gotta do is sink your teeth in Alberto's butt and not let go. Forget about those other guys and forget about your time. Do not go to the lead during the first 10 miles no matter how good you feel. Just tuck in with the lead pack and enjoy the scenery. Never let Alberto get more than a C-hair away from you. Then when you get to the hills . . . aw hell, Dickie, you know what to do on the hills. Good luck, kid. See ya back in town."

They shook hands again, and then the coach was gone. A few minutes later, at 11:45 a.m., Dick gathered his gear and said thanks and good-bye to his hostess. Then he jogged out to the street, heading for the section at the front of the starting area roped off for elite athletes. But before he got very far, he was stopped in his tracks: Thousands of citizen-athletes stood between him and the starting line. The runners had moved down from the high school staging area and were now massed on the green, spilling down toward the gate of pine trees at the starting line. More than 6,000 people—stretching and bouncing, adrenaline-stoked and gimlet-eyed, sweating and farting—stood between Beardsley and his destiny.

He had blown it. He had worked like a plow horse for 4 months, he had run up and down hills in a blizzard, he had pounded his quads into jerky in front of Johnny Carson, and now, due to his own screwup, he was not going to get to the line on time. He was Dick Beardsley, the son of drunks from Wayzata, Minnesota, who hadn't even made it to the state cross-country championships when he was in high school, who'd ridden out to the starting line looking backward like a 9-year-old.

Beardsley panicked. He felt as if he were caught in one of those sweat-drenched nightmares in which he was desperately trying to reach a critical destination but couldn't move. (Decades later, after detox, Beardsley will be haunted by a similar nightmare: He's been in another accident. He's lying in a hospital bed, and nurses are hooking him up to an IV-drip attached to a huge bag of Demerol. He tries to scream at the nurse to stop, but not a word comes out of his mouth.)

So Dick reverted to character. He started to make noise. "Hey, let me through! I'm Dick Beardsley, for crying out loud! I gotta get up to the front!"

The other runners, immersed in their last-minute preparations, eyed him coldly. Then someone recognized him, and word rippled through the crowd. "Look out; we got Dick Beardsley here! Make way; Dick's coming through!"

The crowds parted, and Beardsley, his nightmare dissolved into a dream, followed a clear path to the starting line.

3

Born in Havana but raised in the Boston suburb of Wayland, Alberto Salazar, the world's most famous distance runner, was coming home from Oregon to run his first Boston Marathon.

As the plane traveled east over the Rockies, Salazar turned restlessly in his seat. Although gratified by the results of the past week, he was also sore and weary. The previous Saturday, April 10, in a 10,000-meter match race with the great Kenyan runner Henry Rono at Hayward Field at the University of Oregon in Eugene, Salazar had run a blistering 27:30, just 2 seconds off Craig Virgin's American record. The 10,000 had been Salazar's idea. He had lined up the appearance fee for Rono, then had gone to almost absurd lengths to make sure that the African showed up to claim it.

The running community thought Salazar was foolish for launching the enterprise, which violated every code in the sport's training canon. A runner was supposed to taper during the 2 weeks before a marathon, cutting back radically on the quantity and quality of his training in order to bring the freshest legs possible to the 26.2-mile race. Mid-April, moreover, was far too early in the spring track season for attempting a personal record, let alone a national one. But Salazar had spent his entire career flaunting the conventional wisdom. At the age of 16, he had determined that he would become the fastest marathoner in the world. Instead of the standard training—laying a foundation of endurance by running long distances at a comparatively slow pace, then adding speedwork—Salazar did the opposite. He first honed his track speed to match that of a Henry Rono, then built his strength so he could maintain that pace over the length of a marathon. His goal was to demolish his competitors, to run so far out in front of them that there could be no doubt of his greatness.

"I viewed every marathon as a test of my manhood," he said. "It wasn't enough for me to win the race. I wanted to bury the other guys."

Last week's 10,000-meter race had occurred on a cold, rainy afternoon, as a special added attraction to a collegiate track meet. The crowd had been large, loud, and knowledgeable. The golden era of University of Oregon distance running had come 7 or 8 years earlier, when the legendary coach Bill Bowerman guided a team featuring the swashbuckling Steve Prefontaine, whose death in a 1975 car accident vaulted him to James Dean–like sainthood. Nearly equaling Prefontaine's passion and at least his equal in talent and accomplishment, Salazar was the central figure in the U of O's silver era. Alberto had been directed to Oregon by his older brother, Ricardo, who had been a miler at Annapolis and was now a fighter pilot serving on an aircraft carrier cruising in the Indian Ocean.

"If you're serious about wanting to be the best," Ricardo had told Alberto, "then you have to go to Oregon." Bill Dellinger, the former University of Oregon and Olympic-medalist distance runner who had succeeded Bowerman as head track coach at the university, traveled across the country to sign Alberto to a scholarship. He had graduated the previous spring but continued to live and train in Eugene, the undisputed distance-running capital of the United States.

The town was abuzz on race day. The match between the two world-record holders elicited the excitement that a big football game would have aroused in Norman, Oklahoma, or a play-off basketball game in Chapel Hill, North Carolina. If Salazar had merely been running the race, he might have been able to enjoy it, but he worried until the starting gun whether Rono would show up.

The negotiations with the Kenyan—who had competed as a scholarship athlete at Washington State University and at that time owned the world record in the 3000, 5000, and 10,000 meters, as well as the 3000-meter steeplechase—began badly. Out of shape and in the early stages of the alcoholism that would cut short one of the most brilliant careers in track and field history, Rono balked at the idea of the race. But Salazar persisted, first by sweetening the pot (a local car dealer put up $2,500 in appearance money), then by threatening Rono with the possibility that Nike, his shoe sponsor, would withdraw support if he failed to cooperate. Rono finally agreed to run. After arriving in Eugene, however, he hinted at his desire for an additional perk: female companionship.

Henry Rono's infamous Rabelaisian appetites were diametrically opposed to those of the vast majority of distance runners in general, and Alberto Salazar—an observant Catholic with strict morals—in particular. As a native Cuban, moreover, Salazar would have found the concept of women for hire especially repugnant. Through much of Cuba's history, American men had played out their erotic fantasies—and exploited poor Cuban women—in Havana bordellos. Indeed, upon assuming power in 1959, one of Fidel Castro's first acts had been to shut down the brothels. Jose Salazar, Alberto's father, had then been a friend and comrade of Castro's. Now Henry Rono was in Eugene fishing around for a massage parlor.

Had Rono explicitly pressed the matter, Salazar very well might have called off the race. On the other hand, Rono was a trail-blazing African athlete and one of the greatest performers in the history of the sport. Salazar wanted to take a shot at the American record in the 10,000 meters, and he knew that no one would be able to push him—or pull him—like Rono, who had engaged Salazar in a number of memorable battles during their undergraduate years. Salazar was also looking ahead to the 1984 Olympics in Los Angeles, in which he planned to run both the 10,000 and the marathon. The 9-day interval between the track race in Eugene and the marathon in Boston was the same as between the two races in Los Angeles. The facts were that Salazar needed Rono and that the latter might have considerable difficulty finding what he wanted in Eugene.

The small Willamette Valley college city was in some ways more puritanical than postrevolutionary Havana. Despite its eco-liberal, Grateful Dead–loving image (or perhaps because of it), Eugene eschewed such old-paradigm debaucheries. Freewheeling, multipositioned, pot-enhanced sex between consenting adults was acceptable—in fact, in many parts of town, it was encouraged—but the kind of professional transaction that Rono seemed to seek was beyond the pale. When Henry muttered something about getting a non-sports medicine-style "massage," Alberto ignored him. The Kenyan then apparently struck off on his own, seeking the districts of Eugene more in line with its earthy sawmill past than save-the-salmon present.

Indeed, Rono had only shown up in Eugene after a sportswriter friend of Salazar's dragged him out of a tavern in Palo Alto, California, where Rono had run in a recent track meet. The sportswriter drove Rono to his hotel to sober up and pack for the flight to Oregon. On the way to the hotel, Rono had leaned out of the car at stoplights, propositioning every woman within hailing distance.

But here he was at Hayward Field (lying at the heart of campus and named in honor of Bill Hayward, the university's first track coach, who, in 1982, had only two successors, Bowerman and Dellinger), looking fat and blowsy from his dissipations. Once the gun sounded, however, Rono ran with his trademark ferocity. For 25 laps around the historic track, the two men belted away at each other. Rono out-leaned Salazar at the wire by the width of his jiggling belly, the wags in the press box joked. Bill Bowerman, who had been among the spectators, called it one of the greatest races he had ever seen.

And yet, even after that draining, world-class effort, Salazar had refused to throttle back his training. A few days later, on another cold, rainy afternoon, he had logged a brutally hard workout consisting of 10 full-speed 200-meter repeats. He developed a sore right hamstring. The pain was nagging rather than debilitating; but in his workouts since his injury, he hadn't been able to achieve full extension in the stride.

Molly, Salazar's wife, sat next to him on the plane. An attractive blonde, a native Oregonian with a manner as relaxed as her husband's was clenched, Molly had been a talented long-distance runner at the U of O. Their marriage was thriving, as was their business partnership. Alberto made $250,000 base salary from Nike, along with prize money and frequent bonuses. Molly handled the financial affairs; Alberto ran.

In sum, it would be difficult to imagine a young man returning home in more triumphant circumstances. In October, he had won his second consecutive New York City Marathon in world-record time. In March, he had finished second at the world cross-country championships in Morocco. The week before, he had run the great race against Rono. He was the prohibitive favorite to win the

Boston Marathon on Monday. Salazar was famous and wealthy, had a loving and beautiful wife, and at age 23 had already met with the president in the White House. With the Great Plains spooling out 37,000 feet beneath the airplane, the world figuratively and literally lay at Alberto Salazar's feet.

And yet, he wasn't satisfied. He felt tired and irritable, much like an overtrained racehorse. His leg ached. For all that he had accomplished, he still thought that he had more to prove. He wasn't a fighter pilot like his brother, and he hadn't waged guerrilla warfare in the mountains of Cuba with Fidel Castro like his father. Alberto was merely the best marathoner in the world, which only meant that he could withstand the most pain. He was not the fastest runner or the prettiest one to look at, but he could run at the red line—that place where speed and pain commingled—longer than anybody on earth. That made him a man of valor like his father, didn't it? Who was this Dick Beardsley? Where did he go to college? Who was his father?

Salazar knew that Beardsley would be his chief threat on Monday. However, Alberto didn't really take him seriously. Beardsley lacked the speed—more important, he lacked the credentials—to truly challenge him. In his remarks to the media, Salazar didn't even mention Beardsley's name. He didn't want Beardsley to think he was in Salazar's league.

As the flight droned on, Salazar felt simultaneously confident and edgy. Most of all, he was exhausted. He looked forward to a quiet, anonymous arrival at the airport, a private reunion with his parents, and a long night's sleep in his own bed.

The flight attendant came down the aisle, rattling the beverage cart. Molly stirred in the seat next to him, then went back to sleep. Molly and Alberto had started dating during his sophomore year, and he had never considered another woman. With his fame and good looks, many women might have pursued him, but Salazar succeeded in keeping people at a distance. He felt at ease only among fellow elite runners, athletes who shared his uncompromising standards. The day he returned to campus after his first New York City Marathon, for instance, the cross-country team had been meeting in the field house with Dellinger. When the athletes saw Alberto, they spontaneously rose for a standing ovation, a moment that he still regarded as one of his highest honors.

But for those outside that circle, Salazar could seem cold and arrogant. He did not suffer fools gladly. In a town and campus full of Reagan-reviling devotees of the 1970s' counterculture, Salazar was a clean-cut conservative who revered the president as an anti-Castro patriot. To the average Eugene woman in her flannel shirt and Birkenstocks, the aristocratic Cuban-American superstar with his young-priest, to-die-for face must have seemed glamorous, exotic, and unapproachable.

The flight attendant offered him a beverage; Alberto shook his head. She gestured to the sleeping Molly, and he shook his head again. The flight attendant continued down the aisle, her hip brushing Alberto's shoulder as she passed. He closed his eyes, hoping for sleep, but instead the events of the week came hurtling over him.

Henry, you've signed a contract, you have to show.

Okay, but I got other requirements.

Look, Henry, you're not going to get another cent . . .

No, Henry said, not money.

Hayward had been wet and gray and bone-cold and he couldn't get warm and Henry was there fat from his beer and the

*final six laps they were all alone trading the lead in the wind and
rain feinting and surging and trying to bury one another but neither succeeding and you could hear the roar coming down from
the stands across the infield. The bell lap came and Alberto started
his last long drive from the backstretch, the pain blading up from
his right hamstring. He could not shake him could not shake him
and on the final turn Henry moved past him and Alberto sprinted,
Dellinger had been working with him on his sprint technique. He
could sprint with Henry Rono yes and he caught up again as the
crowd screamed and the rain and wind drove off of the Pacific but
in the last meters Henry summoned his pride speed toughness to
out-lean him at the wire.*

The jet blasted toward Boston in the darkness. Cranky and uncomfortable after the long flight with no sleep, his hamstring tight-
ening and his feet swelling, Salazar again longed for a quiet arrival.

"I gave my father express orders," he told Molly. "No reporters at the airport."

"That's good," she said, now awake and leafing through the
airline magazine. "Think he'll follow through?"

"He better."

Molly said nothing.

"We'll go straight home, get a good night's sleep. Tomorrow I'll
go for a few easy miles and stretch out this hamstring."

"How about the media?"

"I'll talk to them, but I'm in no big rush."

In other words, since the Boston Marathon refused to pay an
appearance fee like other major road races, Salazar would not ex-
tend himself with the journalists. For nearly a century, with the
quadrennial exception of the Olympics, Boston was the only pres-
tigious marathon in the world; marathoners had no choice but to

come to it. During the 1970s, however, many major cities around the world founded marathons, and most offered prize money to professional athletes. Steeped in tradition, clinging to its former privileged status, Boston refused to engage in a bidding war for talent with its new competitors. The race remained stubbornly amateur. Its reputation still drew plenty of accomplished citizen-athletes, but world-class performers increasingly skipped Boston in favor of the paydays offered by marathons such as Rotterdam, Chicago, and New York City. Salazar was doing Boston a huge favor by simply showing up. He saw no need to sell the marathon through extensive media interviews.

"I just don't see why I should become some sort of overly out-going media-type personality just because that will make it easier for people to interview me or the public to have access to me," Salazar had complained in a recent article in the *Boston Globe*.

Therefore he had instructed his father: no reporters at the airport. None of that soppy, come-home-again junk. All of the ritual claptrap accompanying the Boston Marathon was of little interest to Alberto. He was a professional, a serious man on a business trip. His concern was the race itself, employing the marathon as a laboratory to test how far he could push his body, mind, and will. The intersection of speed and pain was where Salazar wanted to dwell, not the tacky sphere of celebrity.

The plane looped over the Atlantic in the April night and vectored down toward Logan. Alberto felt seriously jet-lagged. His jeans were rumpled, his mouth was cottony, and his hamstring twinged. Molly looked equally haggard.

Down the jetway into the arrival lounge and the first camera popping . . . wait a minute . . . another pop. Alberto! Hey Alberto! Joe Concannon from the Globe *holding a notebook. Alberto, got*

a minute? The guy in a blazer from WBZ, he couldn't re-
member . . . just a quick stand-up, Alberto.

There were blinding TV lights and behind them radio mikes
and more newspaper guys. Dad had told. There he was, standing
against the wall. Alberto just caught a glimpse of him, like when
he was a kid in his bedroom and the voices were loud downstairs
and Alberto came down to find the strange men filling the dining
room, cigar-smoking Spanish-speaking men of valor, of El Exilio,
all listening to his father.

Alberto, what are your thoughts about coming home to run
Boston?

The lights were on, the cameras rolling. Molly had slid out of
sight to join his father. The pens were poised over the notebooks.
Damn it to hell there was nothing else but to be a professional,
step into the light.

"There's no other runner here who especially concerns me. . . . If
there are no injuries or unforeseen developments . . . well, the facts
are plain; I'm the fastest man in the race."

The lights went dark, and Joe Concannon shook his hand
half-apologetically, the way reporters do when they're trying to
ingratiate themselves. Concannon was the veteran running-beat
reporter from the *Globe,* an old-school, bar-stool kind of guy like
Bill Squires. Concannon, Jose, Molly, and Alberto walked
through the terminal, making small talk, then Joe said, "So long,"
and shuffled off to his car. Jose, Molly, and Alberto proceeded to
baggage claim, collected the luggage, and continued to the
parking garage. Not until they were inside of Jose's car did
Alberto cut loose.

"I told you not to tell any reporters I was coming in, and look what happens!"

"I only told Joe," Jose Salazar replied. "How would I know he'd go blabbing and ruin his scoop? Anyway, you did fine. Molly, you look lovely, sweetheart. How was the flight?"

"Only told Joe! Why didn't you just announce it on WBZ and print invitations!"

Then they were off, engaged in an all-out, daggers-drawn battle all the way to Wayland, as bad as in the old days when Alberto was a teenager, so bad that Molly cringed in the backseat and Alberto ordered his father not to take them home. He refused to sleep under his father's roof.

"All right, mister big shot. If that's the way you want it."

They went to a fleabag motel in Wayland, the closest one to the house. Jose drove away angrily. Alberto angrily checked in and stomped to the room with Molly in his wake. Seething, jet-lagged, his hamstring throbbing, Alberto threw off his clothes and got into bed. *Big mouth father sorryass motel Joe Concannon my butt.* He flicked out the lights, settled in. But the sheets felt itchy. He flipped over, but the sheets were still itchy. It felt like ants were crawling up and down his legs. Alberto flicked on the light, drew back the sheets. They were ants! A million frigging ants in this fleabag motel room!

Alberto leaped around the room, cursing and smashing ants with his shoe. Molly drew away, not knowing whether to laugh or cry.

4

At mile 5, the lead pack passed a pond where a couple was floating around in a canoe, enjoying the beautiful afternoon. Bill Rodgers poked Beardsley. "Hey, Dick, wouldn't you love to be out there right now?" He spoke as if they were two young executives commuting into the office, looking out the train window.

Dick started to relax. He was thrilled to be running beside Rodgers, four-time winner of the Boston Marathon and three-time winner at New York City. They had met under memorable circumstances at the New York City Marathon in '80. While rounding a tight turn in Brooklyn, Beardsley and Rodgers tangled legs, and Rodgers took a tumble. After the race, Rodgers, feigning anger, had mock-strangled Beardsley. Meanwhile, all the reporters flocked around Salazar, the newly crowned champion and Rodgers's former teammate on the Greater Boston Track Club.

Indeed, at the Boston starting line a few minutes earlier, Beardsley had had another one of his starstruck, lost-little-boy moments. Rodgers stood on one side of him, and Salazar—not even deigning a glance, let alone a handshake—on the other. Beardsley's heart sank—he was little Dick from Wayzata who rode out to the starting line looking backward like a 9-year-old. But then he took a few deep breaths. He looked again at Salazar, recalling his

31

arrogance during the TV interview: *There's no other runner here who especially concerns me.* Damn right I belong here, Beardsley thought.

Moments before the start, Barney Klecker, a marathoner friend of Beardsley's from Minnesota, approached. "Good luck, Dick."

"Thanks, Barney. Same to you."

"Did you double-tie your shoelaces?"

"What?"

"Your shoelaces. Did you double-tie them?"

Dick looked down. "My shoelaces are fine, Barney."

"You should always double-tie them. If you took a moment to do it now, it might save you a lot of grief later on. I know of more than one runner who lost a race because his shoelace became untied."

"Barney, for crying out loud, my shoelaces are fine." The race was going to start in less than a minute. Salazar was already moving forward. Dick started to follow him, but he stumbled over something: Klecker was kneeling on the ground, double-tying Dick's shoelaces, adding another surreal note to the day and forging still another connection to Beardsley's humble heartland roots.

Finally the cannon boomed, and the runners started down Route 105, headed toward Ashland, the next town on the point-to-point course through the Boston suburbs. "Down" was more than a figure of speech: Over its first 16 miles, the course dropped from an elevation of 462 feet to 49 feet; over the first mile, it plunged more than 100 feet. Pine trees jutted close to the sides of the two-lane highway. There were kids halfway up the trees and people out in lawn chairs in the sunshine with their coolers.

Anxious to avoid getting caught in the stampede of the start, Alberto took off as if he were a football receiver running a fly pattern. Dick followed. He was not going to let Alberto out of his sight. They passed the first mile in a ludicrously fast 4:38, then settled down to a steady 5-minute-per-mile pace. A lead pack formed—Salazar, Rodgers, Ron Tabb, Dean Matthews (with whom Dick had shared an apartment in Atlanta over the winter), Ed Mendoza, and Beardsley. The pack served an important function during the early stages of a marathon, allowing the top athletes to maintain pace and share the burden of blunting headwinds. It formed a type of refuge within which the contenders could appraise themselves and each other, watch and wait, and husband their energy for the hard racing to come.

Beardsley did not feel his best over those early miles. He had drunk a great deal of water, and now it sloshed around in his belly. His legs felt heavy, and he couldn't hit an easy rhythm. But the first part of a marathon was frequently difficult. Dick knew that the water would soon be absorbed and his limbs would loosen. He intimately understood the 26.2-mile distance. He'd already run 15 marathons, everything from the Paavo Nurmi Marathon in Hurley, Wisconsin, to the Beppu Marathon in Japan. He'd run each of his first 13 marathons faster than the previous one, an achievement that put his name in the *Guinness Book of World Records*. Dick might not be as fast as Salazar, he might not be able to touch Alberto on the track, but Dick was significantly more experienced in the marathon.

"Every marathon I ran, I knew I had a faster one in me," Beardsley recalled. "Even though I'd be spent, even though I'd be cramped up, I knew with a little more training, a little more preparation, a little more experience, I could run faster. . . . The tables had turned. It used to be I'd see a Garry Bjorklund [a national-class marathoner from Minnesota who had mentored Beardsley] in a race and almost give up before it started. Now I was the guy people were watching."

The sun hammered down, and the hot asphalt burned through the thin soles of his racing flats. Salazar ran just to his right, close enough to touch. Twelve more miles—just about an hour—until the hills. Twelve more miles to watch, wait, and not let Alberto escape. Beardsley felt enormously relieved to be finally racing. He was glad he'd drunk all that water. In another hour, he knew, he'd be gladder still.

"Hey, Dick, wouldn't you love to be out there right now?" It was odd—Rodgers had known Alberto much longer than he'd known Beardsley, but it was Dick he'd joked around with.

Then a few miles past the pond, in a significant breach of marathon etiquette, Tabb and Matthews threw a rogue surge, abruptly bolting ahead of the lead pack. It was way too early for a serious ante, but not so early that the contenders could afford to ignore it. They had to burn precious energy reeling in the pair. Hemingway would have called the stunt a sloppy way to fish. Beardsley laughed it off, but Salazar was genuinely steamed. "What are those jerks doing?" he snarled.

The crowds were thick along the roadway. The Boston Marathon formed a 26.2-mile-long block party. Dick saw beer kegs, barbecue grills, girls in halter-tops, their winter-white bellies turned to the sun. There were no barricades; spectators could press as close as they wanted to the runners.

Most of the crowd cheered for Salazar, the native son. They assumed that Salazar had arrived to fill Rodgers's shoes, continuing the royal line of home-grown Boston Marathon champions.

Dick decided to have a little fun with the locals. When Salazar waved at his fans, Beardsley did likewise. He waved and grinned as if this were the Fourth of July parade back home in Rush City, and the folks were cheering for him. Salazar was not amused.

Alberto wasn't finding much of anything amusing. He was

booming along in the lead pack, looking strong, yet Beardsley sensed that he wasn't quite in sync. "The only thing I can remember thinking during the first few miles was something Rodgers had said," Salazar told reporters afterward. "I always claim that the marathon is just another race to me. But Billy insists that someday the marathon can humble you. I thought about that in the first 4 miles. 'Could this be the race that gets me?' I could feel the knot in my hamstring, and I started to think, 'Gee, this must be what Rodgers is talking about.' Here my leg was hurting, and I still had 22 miles to go."

Beardsley also noticed that, despite the glaring sun and 70-degree temperatures, Salazar never drank. There weren't any official, fully stocked water stations. You had to accept cups of whatever a spectator might offer. As often as he could, Dick would grab a cup, pour whatever it contained over his painter's cap, take a swallow, then offer the cup to Salazar. But he always refused it.

5

On the morning of November 13, 1989, snow was forecast for Chisago County in the dairy-farm belt of eastern Minnesota, just across the St. Croix River from Wisconsin. In the late 19th century, the area was settled by immigrants from Sweden, peasant farmers to whom the privations of the new land paled in comparison to the poverty and tyranny of the old country. Centered around Lake Chisago, the region formed the setting for the Swedish novelist Vilhelm Moberg's epic series *The Emigrants*. During the late 1940s, Moberg spent parts of each summer researching his books, bicycling from his base in Chisago City to visit the local farmers. The novels continue to be read avidly in Sweden, where, thanks to Moberg, schoolchildren are more familiar with Chisago County than any other part of America. In *The Settlers*, published in 1956, the author describes the country in autumn. "The shores of Lake Ki-Chi-Saga were most beautiful in the fall, when the colors of the deciduous trees mingled with the pines," Moberg wrote. "In the evenings enormous flocks of wild geese flying southward stretched over the lake. The birds up there knew what to expect and moved in good time; winter was near."

Now that the leaves were down, you could see the edge of Lake Chisago from Bloom Lake Farm, which Dick Beardsley leased from the grandson of the Swedish pioneers who had cleared and built the place. Before the storm arrived, Beardsley, recently retired from his professional running career, needed to milk his herd of 45 Holsteins, store the feed corn that he'd harvested the day before, and pick the corn remaining in his fields. He rose at a quarter to 4, blitzed through milking, skipped breakfast, and went to work loading the harvested corn in a grain elevator.

Dick worked at the far end of the barn, near the elevator, using a tractor engine to power the grain auger. To transmit energy to the auger, he employed a device called the power takeoff, or PTO, a revolving steel rod connected to the tractor engine. At 9:00 a.m, he was already 5 hours into his workday. A neighboring farmer was on his way to help him harvest the rest of the corn, and Dick wanted to be ready for him. Such hectic and exacting moments were the rule in dairy farming, but Dick had always relished the life. The attraction was odd, because he hadn't grown up on a farm. His father was a traveling salesman for a line of women's apparel. Bill Beardsley covered a territory encompassing the entire Upper Midwest, often staying away from home for weeks at a time.

"My dad could sell anything," Beardsley recalled. "He could walk into a room full of strangers, and in 5 minutes everybody would be his friend. Dad was a good provider. You could say that about him, if not a whole lot else."

Bill Beardsley also loved to fish. He first took Dick out on a lake when the boy was 3 years old. When his father was sober and in an agreeable mood, they would hook up their boat to the car and drive out to northwestern Minnesota, which was closer to Winnipeg than the Twin Cities and where hundreds of the state's famous 10,000 glacial lakes teemed with walleye, the region's prize catch. These fishing trips formed the fondest memories of Dick's boyhood.

When Dick was 6 or 7, his father embarked on one of his long business journeys. The boy missed him so much that he wouldn't come out of his room, and his mother had to call the pastor from Wayzata Lutheran Church to visit the house and talk to him. When his father returned home, he was told the story and, in an effort to reconnect with the boy, took Dick camping. Despite his fondness for fishing, Bill, unfortunately, wasn't much for roughing it. He failed to set the tent up properly, and when it rained that night, the tent—along with the man and boy inside of it—washed down a hill. That ended the camping trips. His father hit the road again.

"To be honest, we were always glad to see him go," Beardsley said. "Because most times when he came back, it wasn't so great. He and Mom would start drinking. They would go out to dinner, which you think would make them happy. But instead they came home screaming at each other. My two sisters and I would have to cover our ears in our beds upstairs."

To escape, Dick would follow the railroad tracks in back of the house through a golf course and into the woods. Wayzata was still a small, self-contained town then and not the bedroom-suburb of the Twin Cities that it is today. Dick roamed the woods, fished nearby Lake Minnetonka for bass, and hunted with his .22-caliber rifle. He taught himself to trap squirrels and rabbits, a skill that he in turn taught his best friend, George Ross, who lived out in the country, a few miles from town. Carole and Joe, George's parents, were like a second mother and father to Dick, providing the stability that he couldn't get at home. Prosperous dairy farms surrounded the Ross place. In the summers, Dick went to work on one. The moment that he settled his ear to the side of a cow, felt the solidity and warmth, breathed the rich commingled aroma of hay, feed, milk, and manure, he knew just what he wanted to do with his life: operate his own small dairy farm.

"I spent most of my free time helping neighboring farmers with their chores," Beardsley wrote in his autobiography. "I fed horses, milked cows, butchered chickens, and cleaned hog barns. Whatever they needed me to do, I did it and didn't complain. I loved it. I was big into 4-H, which my parents thought was hilarious. . . . They were city folk who somehow gave birth to a farm kid."

Cows fascinated Dick. He studied the animals tirelessly and experimented with them, piecing together the optimal feed mixtures and conditions that would produce top outputs of milk. Milk production was how you made money and won the respect of your neighbors, the two things that mattered most to a good dairy farmer. The county co-op kept exact daily, weekly, and monthly totals for each farm and cow. You knew precisely where you stood compared to the other farmers. It was highly competitive, just like running. In fact, dairy farming and distance running were alike in more ways than they differed.

In June 1979, Dick married Mary Hausmann, from Bonesteel, South Dakota, a fellow student at South Dakota State. Although he was a hungry reader possessed of a keen native intelligence, Beardsley was never much of a scholar; cross-country and track appealed to him considerably more than academics. He had been a good collegiate runner, but there seemed no hope of making a living at the sport. When the opportunity arose to lease a spread near the town of Redwood Falls in southwestern Minnesota, Dick thought he should take it. He would put away childish things, forget about college and running, and earn a real living for his bride. "Mary's parents weren't farmers, but a lot of her aunts and uncles were," he explained. "So when we started talking marriage, family, and future, the plans were always set against the backdrop of a dairy farm."

Beardsley went out alone to the farm while Mary got a job in town. The farm turned out to be a miserable place, run-down and filthy, with a mangy, threadbare herd of milkers. It was winter, and Dick missed Mary and his friends. One night, he opened a copy of a running magazine and saw that the qualifying standard for the '80 Olympic marathon trials wasn't far beyond his reach.

The next day, it was freezing cold at 4:00 a.m., and Dick was alone in the stinking barn with the shitting cows. The place was a mess. Everything needed to be done. He suddenly burst into tears. He was an emotional man who always cried easily, but who wouldn't cry in that situation? As soon as he finished milking, he packed his pickup, left the farm, fetched Mary, drove to the Twin Cities, found an apartment and a part-time job at Foot Locker, and started training for the marathon trials. From that point forward, his running career streaked by in a blur. It seemed like just a matter of weeks until he was racing over the Newton Hills at the Boston Marathon next to Alberto Salazar—and just a few more weeks until he was undergoing surgery on his Achilles tendon and his professional career was finished. Ten years after he'd walked away from the farm, Beardsley was thinking about cows again.

He didn't have the money for a place of his own, so he got a job in South Dakota working as a field agent for the Land O'Lakes dairy-food company. He would drive a circuit of dairy farms, talking to farmers about their herds and suggesting improvements to the bovine diet. He had a company car, a steady income with benefits, and a house in town. Dick loved it and so did Mary, who never cared for the hard-core farming life. Still, he felt a pang when he visited a farm, inspected the setup, and fantasized about what he could do if he were running it. "If you ever go on vacation and need somebody to milk for you, call on me," he told his customers, and he wasn't joking.

Time passed and Dick continued to pine, reading *Hoard's Dairyman* like he once read *Track and Field News.* One day, he noticed an ad for a farm near Lake Chisago in Minnesota, not far from the St. Croix River and the trails he used to run when he and Mary were living in the log cabin near Rush City. Dick drove over to take a look. It was the most god-awful run-down place he ever saw, worse than the farm he'd walked away from a decade ago. It was weedy and flyblown and dilapidated; there were rusty car hulks in the ditches, and the barn was practically falling down. But even in its present state, Dick saw that it had once been a fine and sustaining place; at 200 acres, it was just the size he imagined for himself.

The property had a nice little lake—Bloom Lake—a stand of woods, and an interesting history. Although he now lived in Golden, Colorado, where he worked as a mining engineer, the owner, Duane Bloom, had been born in the farmhouse. Vilhelm Moberg once had coffee in the kitchen, when he'd visited to gather material for his novels. Duane started working on Dick, Dick started working on Mary, and, long story short, in September 1989, Dick quit his job with Land O'Lakes. He and Mary gave up the company car, steady salary, and house in town to move out to Bloom Lake Farm and milk the 45 Holsteins on a potentially profitable but risky lease agreement.

Now, 8 weeks later, he needed to run the corn through the auger and into the elevator and be ready when John came to help get the rest of the corn in before it snowed. Even a little bit of snow could be ruinous. If you put the corn up wet, it would mold; and come the middle of the Minnesota winter when you fed that corn to the cows, it would turn to mush on your shovel. Also, moldy corn could upset a cow's delicate digestive system. A sour-stomached cow wasn't happy. Dick wanted happy cows because they were better milkers and because making people and animals happy was ingrained deeply in his nature. He could not abide anger or discord. On some farms, the angry, resentful farmer would have his cows so terrorized that they would tremble and shit as soon as they saw him in the barn door. That was not the way to build a blue-ribbon herd. Within a couple of days, all the cows at Bloom Lake Farm loved Dick, although right now he was not in a lovable mood.

He was busting to get the corn in and to prove that he could turn the farm around and make it pay. There was a lot to live up to and not much time. The first flakes of snow were already filtering down through the meager sunlight. Dick couldn't see the stand of woods to the east of the barn where he'd taken his dog just a few days before. To the north, Bloom Lake was also hidden. Mary worked in the milk house, at the opposite end of the barn, cleaning up after morning chores. The tractor made a terrible racket—for the power takeoff to function, you had to run the tractor engine at full throttle. There were two tractors on the place, the small John Deere with the PTO lever in the back and a bigger, newer rig with the lever in the front.

Machinery wasn't Dick's strong suit. He was an animal man. He could just about handle the basics with a machine. If anything went seriously wrong, he would haul the thing to a mechanic in the nearby town of Shafer, then hustle back to his herd, which was already showing progress. The milk yield was up. Dick had sold off some calves (without telling Duane in Colorado) and used the money for new pipes in the barn. He had cleared the weeds out of the ditches. Mary had planted bulbs on the south side of the house.

For the job of storing corn, Dick had chosen the older, smaller tractor, whose PTO turned at 540 revolutions per minute, which translated to 9 revolutions per second. Developed during the 1920s, the PTO was a simple yet remarkably useful and versatile device; virtually every machine on a family farm, from mowers to posthole diggers, ran off of it. The PTO consisted of a 2-foot-long steel shaft with a U-joint on the tractor end and a coupler on the implement end. Protective sleeves fitted over the joint and coupler, but most farmers, including Beardsley, disengaged them. The sleeves fitted awkwardly on older tractors and were often a nuisance.

Dick fastened the coupler to the auger, which would pump the corn—shelled out in the field by the combine—from a wagon into the cylindrical, 30-foot-high grain elevator. Had he used the larger tractor, Dick would have had to start both the engine and PTO from the tractor seat. But since the PTO lever on this tractor was in the back, he could stand on the drawbar and simultaneously engage the PTO and auger, thereby saving a few seconds. For his whole life he'd been in a hurry, trying to save seconds—what else was distance running but moving from the start to the finish a few seconds faster than the next fellow?

With his left foot on the drawbar, right foot in the air, he stretched out to push the lever to start the PTO revolving at 540 rpm. As he did so, his foot slipped. It was a dark morning, spitting snow, Dick was in a hurry, there was corn to get in, and more snow and corn were on the way. His foot slipped as he was leaning forward. It was very cold and gray, and the drawbar was slick with melted snow. Something clouted Dick from behind. He fell to the ground. The thing struck him again. His first thought was that some wild man had wandered off the highway to attack him. Dick slammed into the ground.

He appeared to be turning around in a circle, tumbling around as if he were inside a clothes dryer. The world was blurred and whirling, and Dick again slammed into the ground. Whatever had caught hold of him wouldn't let go. He kept belting into the hard, packed dirt of the barnyard. It was cold and gray, and somebody or something was attacking. Dick looped and slammed. In a horrifying flash, he realized his predicament: When he'd slipped on the drawbar, he had inadvertently started the PTO, and his overalls leg had caught in the U-joint of the revolving shaft. His left leg was curled around the shaft like a string around a spool. Dick orbited along with the shaft, hammering into the ground with each revolution.

PTO accidents have killed an average of a farmer a year in Minnesota and maimed dozens more. Women have caught their hair in an unprotected U-joint or coupler, and the powerfully revolving shaft has torn the tops of their heads off. Kids have caught their fingers in the shaft and have had their arms ripped from their shoulders. But PTO accidents always happened to someone else, farmers who weren't as quick or agile or as fortunate as Dick Beardsley. Yet here he was with his leg wrapped around the shaft, flying around in circles, his skull walloping the frozen ground like a rag doll's.

Dick screamed for help, but Mary was inside the barn, cleaning up after milking, and couldn't hear him. He would have to turn the lever off himself. With each revolution, he clawed desperately for the lever, but it remained just beyond his grasp. There was about a 24-inch clearance between the shaft and the ground, and with each revolution, Beardsley trash-compacted into that space. Theoretically, he was whipping around 9 times a second. He wasn't going that fast because his weight slowed the shaft, but he was still wailing.

He hollered for Mary. She had to hear him. Any moment now, she would come out of the barn and head back to the house. She would glance to her right and see his predicament and rush over and flip the lever. She would help Dick to his feet and brush him off, and they would have a good laugh about it. He would go into

45

the house for a diet soda and a bite to eat; then John would arrive, and the two men would go out to the field to bring in the rest of the corn. Dick would describe his close call. John would say, "Oh sure, you gotta watch those darn PTOs."

But Mary would not come out of the barn. Dick swung around in circles, smacking into the dirt like a damn fool. He was a damn fool. He was Dick Beardsley from Wayzata, a son of two drunks. Once he could run marathons as well as anybody in the world, but those days were gone. Now he was back where he belonged—on a farm with his leg wrapped around a PTO shaft, flying around in terrible circles.

Dick reached for the lever, but it remained just beyond his grasp. He kept reaching as if he were a kid again at the Excelsior Amusement Park on Lake Minnetonka, grabbing for the ring on the carousel. Dick would ride the carousel with his sister, Maryann. Their mother took them to the park once every summer as a special treat. Or this was like the time when Dick and Joe Ross went out on a snowmobile to help the lady on the neighboring farm during a blizzard. On the way back, they got lost in the woods, and it took Joe a long time to find their way in the snow. For a moment, Dick, who was only 14 at the time, was sure they were lost for good. Or it was like the last few miles of the Boston Marathon, when Dick couldn't feel his legs anymore and he and Alberto Salazar seemed corded together by invisible bands, pushed along by some powerful, unseen hand.

Beardsley blasted around the PTO shaft. He felt no pain. He could not reach the lever. Mary was in the barn and couldn't hear him screaming. Dick couldn't hear himself. Maybe he wasn't screaming at all, like in a nightmare when you tried to scream but couldn't make a sound.

He felt numb and calm. He was floating a few feet above the

barnyard, watching himself slam around in these awful crazy circles. It was kind of interesting. It was dark and cold and a little snow was falling. Dick liked this sort of weather; he liked any kind of weather. Now the morning was brightening, which was odd because the snow still fell and there was no sign of the sun. The light kept getting brighter. Mary was in the barn. He could not reach the lever.

Somehow, the tractor engine died. The drag of his weight must have slowed the old tractor engine to the extent that it finally stalled. The PTO shaft stopped turning, and Dick was no longer flying around in circles. He felt no pain, but the strange brightness still illuminated the yard. Mary remained in the milk house. He was too weak to call to her. She wouldn't have heard him anyway because of the pumps and compressors in the milk house and the bellowing of the herd in the barn. A farm was a god-awful noisy place. The idea that you could find peace and quiet in the country was a joke.

He pulled his pants leg out of the PTO's U-joint. That's all it was. Nothing to it. He unwrapped his leg from around the shaft, which was also surprisingly easy. The leg unwound like a long, limp string of link sausage. But there was no pain, so why not go ahead and stand up, walk across the yard to the house? Dick did stand for an instant, but then he was lying back on the ground with the sausage-link leg coiled numb and smashed beneath him. He would have to crawl to the house.

It was 60 yards or so across the packed, frozen dirt of the yard from the north end of the barn to the small turn-of-the-century frame farmhouse. Although the house needed a coat of paint, it was still a good, tight house that had sheltered generations of tough, pious Swedish farmers who understood how frightening and terrible the new world could be. In the deep north woods, an axe could slip and slice off your foot, you could fall through ice on the lake, a tree could topple over on you, an Ojibway warrior's hatchet could cleave your skull like a grapefruit, or a timber wolf like the legendary Three-Legged Jack, 9 feet long from the tip of his cold nose to the end of his bushy tail, could spring from the shadows and rip your throat out. So the settlers hacked out their homesteads from the pinewoods on the lakeshore, and soon more settlers made their way from the same small Swedish villages. The settlers built Lutheran or Catholic churches according to their histories and then built tidy little towns around them. Post offices, hardware stores, mills, feed stores, cafés—places where people could gather against the terrifying new country—sprang up. The farms and towns prospered. Big families filled the houses like the one Mary and Dick now lived in.

The house lay just across the yard, but it might as well lie across the expanse of Lake Chisago. It might as well be another marathon Dick had been called to run. In a marathon, you never thought about the finish, only about the mile you were presently covering. You took one step at a time, like in the late stretches of the '82 Boston. Dick disciplined himself not to look at the house. He focused on crawling. There was no pain, thank God; and thank God he hadn't been working inside the barn, where the concrete floor would have crushed his skull like an eggshell on the PTO's first go-round. Dick crawled, using his elbows for locomotion, throwing one out in front of his body and using the other for support. His legs dragged behind, the strong whole right one and the left leg that he would think about later. First the right elbow forward, then the left. He did not look at the house, but studied the square inch of dirt in front of his nose as if he were a bug or a snake.

Dick was halfway across the yard when Mary found him. The ambulance came and took him to the small community hospital in Chisago City. Dick was awake through the whole process. In fact, he even cracked a joke with the paramedics, and he joked as well with the nurses in the emergency room. The nurses laughed along with him; people always laughed and smiled when they saw Dick Beardsley. Then the doctor came, and they cut away his clothes and saw the extent of his injuries. The nurses stopped laughing. They wouldn't look him in the eye. Dick felt a stab of fear. And on the heels of the fear, from a place that didn't seem like his leg but a place beyond his leg, he felt the first cold touch of pain.

Things moved very quickly then. They took him to a room and hooked him up to an IV-drip as the pain spread like black floodwater and panic rose in Dick's chest. He knew how to handle pain; he was a marathoner, after all, which was another way of saying he was a pain wizard. But this was something different. This was black and cold and overwhelming. The nurses had him hooked up to a bag of clear liquid that looked like his dad's gin. What could that watery stuff do against the black pain massing up from his mangled leg, punctured lung, fractured wrist, broken ribs, severe concussion, and cracked vertebrae?

But just as the black tide was about to swallow him whole, the Demerol molecules washed over his brain's opioid receptors. Dick rocketed into a new, wonderful world. A world of float and dazzle and laughter and light and peace and no strain, no worry, no corn to get in, no seconds to save, no falling-down Swedish farm with 9-foot-long timber wolves prowling the woods to tear you limb from limb and PTOs spinning in the yard to do the same. Nothing nothing nothing but pure joy. Never in his days had Dick experienced anything remotely like this. Mindful of his parents' example, he had never touched alcohol and never considered recreational drugs, not even marijuana.

The Demerol hit him harder than the packed, frozen earth of the barnyard. Here was truth and light, something so infinitely more pleasing than farming or fishing or running as to be laughable. This was home. It was so wonderful that if some higher power told him he could go back, avoid the accident, but never take Demerol, Dick wouldn't hesitate—he would turn down the offer flat.

6

Near the midpoint of the marathon, the lead pack passed through the notorious gauntlet of shrieking Wellesley College women, who, in the newspaper stories of past races, were described as "shrieking coeds."

Girls not women, lipstick makeup girls screaming at the men as they passed but not really giving a damn about the men, the girls screaming for and at each other, in full shrill throat, venting pent-up New England winter steam-heat frustration, a dense reverberating wall of sound, like Zulu women ululating on the hot road to Durban, raging gleeful keening, a deep true sound to be reckoned with and not just college girls larking as it seemed in the photos. The runners grinned as they first entered the gauntlet, smiling with cocksure pleasure like men paddling into tame riffling rapids, but the deeper they penetrated into the chute of college women the smiles vanished like the grins of kayakers vanished as the tame rapids faded and the boiling white-water loomed.

Past the 13-mile mark at Wellesley, the lead pack melted down to Rodgers, Mendoza, Beardsley, and Salazar. If 1972 Olympic marathon gold medalist Frank Shorter had delivered American distance running to international prominence, then Billy Rodgers was the people's hero, the man who brought marathoning to the masses. A promising runner at Wesleyan University, Rodgers had been a conscientious objector during the Vietnam War and gave up the sport during his CO service at a state mental hospital. While watching the '73 Boston Marathon, however, his interest in running rekindled. He resumed training with the Greater Boston Track Club, under Squires's guidance, and in 1975 won the first of his four Boston Marathon titles. Slight, light-boned, long-haired, Rodgers ran with an effortless, birdlike stride and when not running displayed an implike, spaced-out charm. Rodgers was the prototypical hippie marathoner, a playful new-age warrior who regarded his sport as a vehicle for transcendence rather than a tool for dominance.

"We ran together frequently, with Bill always a half-stride behind, eyes nearly closed, right arm flapping and light hair bouncing rhythmically to the cadence of the run," recalled Amby Burfoot, the '68 Boston champion and Rodgers's roommate at Wesleyan. "It was his relaxation that most amazed me. He seemed to be able to run with almost complete detachment from the mental and physical effort involved."

But at age 34, Rodgers had cut his hair and lost a step. The front-running Mendoza would inevitably fade. The only concern was Beardsley, who Salazar pegged as a talented journeyman. True, he'd run a few good marathons—the 2:09:36 at last June's Grandma's Marathon in Duluth (as if something first-rate could come out of such a backwater, Salazar well might have thought) and the victory at the inaugural London Marathon the previous spring. Actually, London had been a provisional win for Beardsley. At the end of the race, he had dueled for the lead with the Norwegian runner Inge Simonsen. In the final mile, instead of pushing until one or the other broke, they coasted in together, holding hands, "sharing" the victory. Many found the gesture heartwarming; Salazar had been disgusted. You ran to win. You ran to destroy the other man. No quarter given, none asked. Those were the terms of the struggle. To demean them with a hand-holding finish was not the act of a serious man. Beardsley, moreover, had no credentials on the track. His best 10-K was a full minute and a half slower than Salazar's own. And look at him there in his silly little painter's cap, slurping water from every kid he passed.

Alberto still hadn't found his rhythm. His hamstring hadn't loosened. He could not achieve full extension in his stride. In both of his New York City victories, he had powered away from the pack at midrace and finished all alone. With those two triumphs, Salazar had set a new standard for the sport. If Rodgers epitomized the intuitive, countercultural runner who had wandered into the discipline of the marathon, then Salazar was the model of the hard-eyed, Reagan-era athlete who had consciously chosen it.

"The marathon had always been a hand-me-down kind of event," Squires explained. "In general, guys went into the marathon because they weren't fast enough at the shorter distances."

By the early 1980s, however, the marathon was no longer a handmaiden. Since Frank Shorter's gold medal at the '72 Olympics, Rodgers's string of wins in Boston and New York, and the best-selling books of marathon proselytizer Dr. George Sheehan, the 26.2-mile distance had become a glamour event. At the start of his competitive running career, Salazar had specifically set his sights on the marathon. Or it might be more accurate to say that the marathon had chosen him. Indeed, destiny had touched Alberto at the very spot he had just run past.

He had been 16 at the time, a skinny high-school junior from Wayland, the suburban town just north of Wellesley. In the early 1800s, Boston's elite families built their country homes in Wayland.

Later in the century, Irish, Italian, and French Canadian immigrants arrived to work in the shoe mills of the town's Cochituate district. During the 20th century, the mills closed and Wayland became a bedroom suburb of Boston. In the late 1960s, when Jose Salazar's civil engineering firm transferred him from Connecticut to Massachusetts, he settled his family in Wayland. The high school had one of the top track and cross-country programs in New England. Jose sought a coach to nurture the talent of his eldest son, Ricardo.

The Salazar family lived in a house on a long block. One day, a neighbor boy laid out a half-mile course around the block and timed himself running it. "Beat this, Ricardo," the boy taunted. Ricardo accepted the challenge. He was 14 and just starting with high school cross-country. Alberto, 4 years younger, tagged along.

Ricardo ran the loop, looked at his stopwatch, and frowned. "Here, Alberto," he said, "you try it." A half mile might as well be a marathon for a 10-year-old, but Alberto was not about to disobey his brother.

He tore off around the corner. Ricardo cut across the middle of the block to meet him on the backstretch. Ricardo called out his time, then ran back to the finish to wait. And wait and wait. Ricardo walked up the course in the opposite direction to find his brother sitting on the sidewalk, his face buried in his arms.

"I can't do it," Alberto said. "It's too hard."

Ricardo was unmoved. "Try again," he said.

Alberto tried two more times, and each time the result was the same: He had to stop halfway around the block. Sitting on the sidewalk, shattered and exhausted, he confessed to Ricardo that he couldn't continue.

"I thought that Alberto wasn't tough enough to be a runner," Ricardo remembered. "He didn't have the moxie."

From that day forward, Alberto's aim in life was to prove his brother wrong. He was tough, too. He had just as much moxie as Ricardo. He started running all the time—around the block, along the marshes by the Sudbury River, in all-comers track meets during the summer. He studied Ricardo, who progressed into one of the top high-school milers in the East and became the first Cuban-American to win an appointment to the naval academy. Alberto resolved to carve a similar mark, to make his father just as proud of him as he was of Ricardo.

Alberto, however, wasn't a natural athlete like his brother. He was skinny and ungainly, all arms and legs, with a running style that was almost painful to watch. His right leg flew out behind him on each stride, and he plunged forward like an old man struggling not to fall over. He would never become a miler, obviously. At school, Alberto tried his best to be like the other kids, but they taunted him, mocking his foreignness. Alberto realized that if he wasn't like Ricardo, then he wasn't like these American boys either. He had to find his own way to prove himself.

In 1972, when he was a 14-year-old high-school freshman, Alberto entered a road race called the Silver Lake Dodge 20-Miler, which started in Hopkinton and followed most of the Boston Marathon course. Running 20 miles seemed as inconceivable to Alberto as running a half mile had been 4 years earlier. But dropping out was even less conceivable. He soldiered through the first 10 miles, but that was all he had. His father followed him in a car. "You don't look so good," Jose said. "You better stop."

"I can't," Alberto replied. Fighting off tears, alternately running and walking the rest of the way, he was able to finish the race. That was the day he discovered his gift.

He did not possess great natural speed, which was purely a physical property, a matter of muscle mass and favorable genes.

But running long distances, Alberto discovered, required only a modicum of speed. What counted more was the ability to hold that speed to the point of exhaustion and beyond, the ability to court pain instead of avoid it. For the distance runner, pain was a stimulus rather than a brake. Mind and will, not muscle and genes, formed his capital. Many athletes could run fast, but only a man of valor could run fast and long, bending pain to his purpose.

Alberto became a standout schoolboy runner, excelling in cross-country and in track distances of 2 miles and longer. He caught the eye of Kirk Pfrangle, who was a postcollegiate runner at the Greater Boston Track Club coached by Bill Squires. One night in the winter of 1975, Pfrangle invited Salazar to a club workout in the field house at Tufts University.

Squires looked at Salazar and said to Pfrangle, jeezus Kirk what'd'ya think I'm running here, a day care center? Go buy that kid an ice cream cone and let's get to work here.

But Pfrangle said, The kid's a runner, Coach.

Squires considered. There was an A-group for Rodgers and the other studs and a B-group where anybody could run. The same workout for both groups, just different speeds. Okay, put him with the B-group and let's go.

He's not a B-group runner, Coach, Pfrangle said.

Jeez all right Kirk but when we have to scrape the kid off the boards, you're the one's gonna have to explain it to his old man.

They started the workout. A hard series of 1000-meter repeats, 10 of them hard hard pace and Alberto hung with the group for the first 5 or 6, then faltered. Squires told him to back off.

Pfrangle begged him to go easy but Alberto ignored them set his face and nearly killed himself staying with the A-group. But he kept up, finished the workout, and from that day forward there was never a question where Alberto belonged.

He trained with the men traveled and raced with the men ate in the diners with the men and when the jokes turned blue the men would laugh and smirk and say hey, cool it, remember we got the rookie with us. The nickname stuck. Alberto was The Rookie. At the 1975 Boston Marathon The Rookie stood along the course at Wellesley near the shrieking college women and watched Bill Rodgers run by on the way to his first Boston triumph. Alberto told his friends I know that guy, I train with that guy, and he told himself the same thing.

A few days later when Pfrangle was driving him to a club workout the rookie announced that one day he was going to win Boston too. He was going to become the greatest marathoner in the world.

Now, 7 years later, the spectators shouted his name and snapped his photo and pointed him out to their children. Bill Rodgers ran beside him. Beardsley was there, too, trained by Squires. Squires would have prepped Beardsley thoroughly on the hills. He would have stressed to Beardsley that he must surge going down the hills, try to break Alberto there, because Beardsley couldn't compete with Alberto's speed at the end of the race.

Salazar, however, had grown up beside this course. Squires had shown him the same tricks that he'd shown Beardsley. When Salazar began running marathons 2 years earlier, he had made a vow to Bill Dellinger that he would never lose over the distance. He was not about to break that vow today. Beardsley would never beat him on the hills. Alberto was faster, tougher, and had prepared more thoroughly. The hills belonged to him.

✸

A few feet away, Beardsley was thinking the same thing. He had spent the winter training in Atlanta, not to escape the northern cold, but because Georgia, unlike Minnesota, had hills approximating Boston's. There he ran relentlessly, sometimes covering 140 miles a week, working out twice a day, with a long run on Sunday of 20 to 25 miles. Living and training with Dean Matthews, winner of the 1979 Honolulu Marathon, Beardsley started each morning with a run. Then he would eat breakfast, get a massage or soak in the hot tub, and take a nap before embarking on an afternoon workout. Stretching and weight lifting followed. Beardsley thrived on the spartan regimen. For the first time in his career, he was focusing all his physical and mental energy on a single race.

In one of their most taxing workouts, oriented toward building speed, Matthews and Beardsley ran a series of "ladders" on the track. The session began with a 3- or 4-mile warmup. Then they would run two 200-meter sprints, followed by two 400s, two 800s, and two 1200s, culminating with a single 1-mile run. That was the first half of the workout. Then they would climb down the ladder in descending order: two 1200s, two 800s, and so on. The final task would be 1 mile, run in a blistering 4:30.

"Every night after dinner I went for a walk for about half an hour," Beardsley remembered in his autobiography. "The walks were a new addition to my training regimen, but they quickly became as important as the long runs. It was time to think, think, think about the task ahead. . . .

"On one of my walks I found a rock. It was round and flat, but there was a piece missing, so it was in the shape of a V—V for victory, I decided. Every night on my walk I stopped. I took the toe of my right shoe and put it in that V. I made sure the rock was where no one else would ever notice it, so it was right there the next evening when I could touch my shoe to it again. After Boston it was just an abyss—that's how much I was putting into this one race."

In early April, he left Georgia to finish preparing in Boston, where he could familiarize himself with the marathon course. Shortly after his arrival, however, a late nor'easter blew into town, bringing heavy snow and a howling wind. Beardsley was scheduled for a key workout on Heartbreak Hill: up one side and down the other, eight times. Squires looked out the window and told him to forget it.

"Come on, Coach, let's give it a try."

"I don't think I can even get us to Heartbreak, let alone have you run there." But Squires finally relented. He drove at a creeping pace through the deserted streets, delivering Beardsley to within 3 miles of Heartbreak.

"For chrissakes, Dickie, look at this snow. Let's go home. You're gonna slip and fall and kill yourself."

"Let me give it a shot, Coach."

Beardsley got out of the car and started running toward Heartbreak. He ran gingerly at first, but after a few steps picked up the pace. It was cold and uncomfortable, certainly, but not nearly as cold or uncomfortable as hundreds of winter workouts that Beardsley had logged in Minnesota. Still hewing to a dairy farmer's routine, he habitually rose early in the morning—as early as 2:30—when the temperature was often 20 below zero or colder, and the wind-chill factor dipped to near surreal levels.

Now, on Heartbreak Hill in Boston (which really wasn't so steep a hill at all, he thought; not nearly as challenging as the hills he trained on in Atlanta), his footprints cut lonesome notches in the unblemished drifts, and the icy wind scorched his eyes. Beardsley closed his eyes, moving on touch and sound and instinct, imagining—knowing—that at this desperate moment, Salazar was running someplace where it was warm.

He completed eight round-trips over Heartbreak, just as planned. At the end of the workout, he quietly reported to Squires that he was ready. The hills belonged to him.

7

n the weeks and months following the 1982 Boston Marathon, Alberto Salazar's decline was so gradual that it barely seemed like a decline at all.

He spent the first days replenishing the 6 liters of fluids that he had lost during the race and trying to convince reporters and himself that the experience hadn't really been that monumental.

Well, maybe the race had been a little tighter than he'd expected. Beardsley ran gamely, no doubt about that. An interesting marathon, but in no way a landmark one. Now, if you'll excuse me, gentlemen, I've got a busy track season in front of me, some races coming up against some real runners. . . .

Well, okay, one last question. Why didn't I drink more than two cups of water during the race? Because that's how much I drank during my other two marathons. I didn't want to slow down to take water. I wasn't aware of myself sweating that much. And, if you fuss around too much with water, you lose your concentration. Yeah, I guess it was a mistake. It was pretty warm out there. In New York next October, I'll make a point of drinking more water during the marathon. Now thank you, gentlemen.

Alberto Salazar continued his 1982 season, during which he aimed to solidify his position as the finest distance runner of his time—superior at distances starting at 5000 meters and superlative in the pain festival of the marathon. As had been the case since he was 16 years old and declaring his ambition to Kirk Pfrangle, Alberto trained in a singular, contrarian manner. Virtually all serious distance runners used a system designed in the 1950s by the New Zealand coach Arthur Lydiard: first building a base of endurance by running long, slow distance—i.e., abundant miles at an aerobic pace—then, once a sufficient base was amassed, running shorter distances at an anaerobic pace. Employing this elegantly simple system, Lydiard developed a group of outstanding New Zealand runners, most notably the Olympic middle-distance champion Peter Snell. Bill Bowerman, the Oregon coach, imported Lydiard's method, adding the idea of alternating strenuous workouts with less taxing ones, which met with great success.

Salazar incorporated some elements of the Lydiard and Bowerman philosophies into his training but challenged others. Most prominently, he reduced the amount of low-speed, base-building mileage and minimized or eliminated the rest phases of training. Rather than differentiating between running hard and running long, in other words, Salazar ran hard *and* long. He thought that the only way to run fast in distance races was to first run fast in shorter races on the track—hence his 10,000-meter race with Rono 9 days before the Boston Marathon. That episode also dramatized his determination to work harder than any other runner in the world.

"If Alberto heard that the Kenyans were out running 5-minute miles at 6:00 a.m., then he had to do the same thing," said one source who had been close to Salazar during his prime. "The idea was to never rest, never be satisfied at his current level of fitness, but to push, push, push."

After Boston, Salazar returned to Eugene to train for the summer track season in Europe. Ostensibly, he was coached by Dellinger, but in fact Salazar worked however he wanted. The word around town was that he would take a workout that Dellinger suggested, then do twice as much.

In Europe that summer, Salazar topped his superb races in Eugene and Boston with a 27:25:61 10,000-meter race in Oslo, Norway, and a 13:11:93 5000-meter performance in Stockholm, both American records for their respective distances. In October, he returned to New York City and won that marathon for the third consecutive year. His time was a few minutes slower than at Boston, but he appeared to be his elegant, imperious self and on schedule for his date with history. He plotted his apotheosis to occur in 2 years' time, at the 1984 Olympics in Los Angeles.

Salazar had qualified for the 10,000 at the 1980 Moscow Games, but the United States had boycotted those Olympics to protest the Soviet invasion of Afghanistan. The '84 Olympics, however, promised to more than make up for that disappointment. On the final evening of the Games, as fireworks soared overhead during the spectacular closing ceremonies, Salazar planned to run all alone into the Los Angeles Coliseum. On American soil, in front of 100,000 spectators and a worldwide television audience, he would win the Olympic gold medal in the marathon. The only detail detracting from the glory of this picture was the likelihood that, in retaliation for America's snub of Moscow in '80, Cuba would boycott the Los Angeles Games. Fidel Castro's passion for sports, however, was well documented. In Havana, *el presidente* would quite likely follow the Olympic marathon telecast. Castro would know perfectly well where Alberto Salazar had been born. Watching Alberto win the race, Fidel would remember the young man's father.

Through that splendid season of running in 1982, however, Salazar privately worried. His problems started soon after the Boston Marathon in April. Before the marathon, he'd relished his workouts, ripping through them with the barest hint of fatigue. He was able to follow hard days and weeks of training with even harder ones; the ceiling for one training cycle became the floor for the next. But after Boston, the workouts yielded less and less pleasure. His legs felt heavy, his breathing shallow. It took him days instead of hours to recover from a maximum effort. As long as his competitive performances hadn't suffered, however, Salazar could easily convince himself that he hadn't made a serious mistake at the Boston Marathon—that despite drinking so little and running so furiously, he hadn't done himself lasting damage. He scoffed at the media for making such a fuss about his "duel in the sun" with Beardsley.

"After Boston, I had my best track season," Salazar pointed out. "Then I won New York City again on a very slow, difficult day. Nobody wanted to lead the race. My foot hurt. I was just glad to get that marathon out of the way and move on to 1983."

That was the year before the Olympics and also the year of the first world track-and-field championships. Salazar's plan was to work on his speed until the world championships in August, in Helsinki, Finland, where he'd compete in the 10,000 on the track. Afterward, he would focus on preparing for the US Olympic marathon trials in May of '84.

While Salazar's training plan was clear, his execution was uncharacteristically flawed. A chink had appeared in his previously immaculate armor. For the first time in his running career, pain whispered a warning rather than an invitation. On the talk shows and in the magazines and self-help books, all the experts said "listen to your pain." That was fine for joggers, Alberto thought, but the marathoner, the man of valor, could not indulge weakness or doubt. Salazar ignored the subtle but unmistakable decline in the quality of his training. Turning a deaf ear to pain, he applied himself even more fiercely to his quest.

In early summer, he was able to string together 4 solid weeks of training leading up to a 10,000-meter race at Hayward Field in Eugene. A few days before the meet, however, he came down with a virus. Dellinger and others advised him to scratch from the race, but Alberto chose to tough it out. He barely broke 28 minutes, his slowest time at that distance in 3 years. He moved on to Europe, taking his nagging cold with him. There, during the weeks before the world championships, the cold blossomed into a severe case of bronchitis. Salazar was so sick that he had to visit a hospital. Pale and weak, he ran a relatively pedestrian 28:07 in the qualifying round of the 10,000 in Helsinki. In the finals, running on fumes, he logged a dismal 28:40, finishing far back in the pack.

For the first time in a major international competition, Salazar had not run worthy of his name. Since his victory at the New York City Marathon a year earlier, he had achieved nothing of consequence. He had suffered nagging injuries and lingering illnesses. The climactic Olympic year of 1984 was now at hand. But if there were grounds for concern, there was also cause for optimism. After all, he had suffered no major debilitating injury and was afflicted by no identifiable malady. He'd endured nothing like the Achilles tendon surgery that had effectively ended Dick Beardsley's career shortly after the '82 Boston Marathon. Of course, in Salazar's opinion, Beardsley had been foolish, running another major marathon just 2 months after Boston. He'd apparently been chasing another paycheck. There was no greater purpose behind Beardsley's risk, as there was behind his own. Beardsley's foolhardiness—his lack of gravitas—had caught up with him. He had blown out his Achilles and now he was through. Alberto, in his own mind, had merely suffered a run of bad luck.

He returned to Eugene to resume training, but he still wasn't himself. The puzzling, worrisome cycle intensified. "I always felt a little bit sick," Salazar said. "My workouts always seemed to be a chore. When before I used to cover a mile interval workout in 4:29 a mile, now it was 4:30. It was just a little bit of a drop-off, but I didn't feel right."

The all-important year of 1984 dawned. At a meet in California early in the year, he put together a first-rate 27:45 10,000 meters, but the next day his foot was sore. Doctors diagnosed a stress fracture. It was April now, just 6 weeks before the Olympic marathon trials in Buffalo, New York. After intense therapy and a regimen of swimming-pool training, Salazar struggled to a 2:12, second-place performance behind winner Pete Pfitzinger. It earned him a berth in the Games, but for Salazar, finishing second—especially in a race restricted to other Americans—was like finishing last.

He still had a chance to redeem himself in Los Angeles. His stress fracture healed, but the malaise lingered all summer. He went to Houston to acclimate to running in the heat. He thought that if he could log a few solid weeks of training, he still might pull out a win in the Olympic marathon. In late July, he ran just under 28 minutes for a 10,000 in Eugene but injured his hamstring in the process. He limped into Los Angeles. Five days before the race, he was still limping. On the final night of the Games, it was Carlos Lopes of Portugal who glided into the Coliseum before the world's admiring eyes, including, perhaps, Fidel Castro's. Salazar finished an exhausted 15th.

"You could say that I choked at the Olympics, but I never quit," he said. "I don't quit. I'm not going to quit. If you quit and drop out, you're always going to have that moment of doubt. I made a vow never to quit in a race, even if I had to walk in."

Alberto hadn't quit, but he clearly had failed. His apotheosis had fizzled miserably. Pain, however, hadn't beaten him. Instead, events conspired so that he could not achieve a productive level of pain. Thus, he thought, there was no dishonor. If he continued to run faithfully, he would surely return to that magic sector where pain and speed commingled. He was only 26, with many marathons and Olympics lying ahead. But why hadn't God sent him a more palpable affliction—one he could see and name and therefore effectively combat? He went home to Eugene and tried to run.

Then the chain of colds began. One heavy cold after another. Deep, racking, bronchitis-style colds, lining up like winter storm fronts off the coast of Oregon. Consistent high-level training became impossible. Physicians were baffled, and no treatment seemed to help. One doctor speculated that Salazar's immune system was seriously compromised, that he'd suffered hormonal damage from all the races in which he'd pushed so hard—especially the 1982 Boston Marathon. Alberto rejected that line of thinking.

The illness and weakness would not abate. Doctors failed to identify his malady, and Salazar, desperate to fight, remained impotent before an invisible enemy. He experienced insomnia and went to the Stanford Sleep Clinic. He visited a cardiologist. He tried training in Kenya. To stay clear of infections spreading from Molly and the couple's baby boy, Antonio, he slept in a bedroom above his garage. Nothing worked. His training grew more labored, his times inexorably slower.

Yet each month or so, he would call a friend and excitedly report that he had his problem figured out, this time for sure. This surgery, that hormone, or a new place to train. He felt wonderful, he reported, and promised that soon he'd be running as well as ever. Better than ever. The old covenant would be restored.

The friends listened patiently, sympathetically, although Alberto worried that he was beginning to sound like the tiresome aunt at Thanksgiving who talks endlessly about her migraines or chronic fatigue syndrome that no specialist anywhere has been able to diagnose. But now she is seeing this hypnotist, this Rolfer, or this aromatherapist who has gotten to the bottom of it. It wasn't a tiresome relative talking about sleep therapy, however; it was Alberto Salazar. Granting him the benefit of the doubt, the world patiently waited for Alberto to reassume the throne he had so bafflingly vacated.

But each month, after the initial excitement accompanying his supposed breakthrough subsided, Salazar would contract another cold, and his running would again decline. Besides his own crushing disappointment, Alberto felt he was letting down others. He worried that he was making a fool of himself. Certainly, had another athlete come to Alberto with the stories he was telling his friends, he would have nothing but contempt for him. But he couldn't stop searching for the answer, couldn't stop hoping that a clear diagnosis and a subsequent recovery were close at hand. It irked him when people kept bringing up Boston, suggesting that running so hard in the heat might have damaged him. That one race against a lucky palooka like Beardsley might have undermined him was unthinkable.

"You can always look back and say, well, if I had done this or that differently, maybe things would have been different," Salazar told a reporter. "But in my case, I think that I was as smart as I could be at the time. At times I may have overtrained, but I truly don't believe my career was ended by overtraining; I'm quite certain of that. You know I didn't just go from breathing perfectly to all of a sudden, in '95, finding out I'd lost 40 percent of what I had. The doctors say it doesn't usually happen that way. You start to become allergic to something for whatever reason; and the first year you're down a couple of percentage points, the next year another few, and gradually it keeps building up."

Salazar had been a business major at the University of Oregon, and he had always possessed an entrepreneurial streak. He had toyed with the notion of opening a sports bar in Eugene— Prefontaine often talked about owning such a place—but then a local investor approached him with a proposal to buy the town's old passenger train station and convert it into a dinner house. Capitalizing on Salazar's fame, the restaurant would draw customers from town and campus, as well as tourists visiting Eugene. In 1987, Alberto accepted the offer and went into business.

Meanwhile, he continued to consult every medical specialist he could think of. A blood test administered by an endocrinologist, for instance, showed that he had low thyroid levels. Salazar was prescribed a drug called thyroxine. He again grew hopeful, thinking that a concrete, quantifiable condition had finally emerged. But, like always, the excitement soon faded. The thyroid meds had no positive effect on his running. The magic bullet that would restore his sport and his sense of himself again failed to surface.

"I kept changing doctors, kept moving on to the next thing. I still hoped for a breakthrough. But I kept getting steadily slower. After '84, I never ran a sub-29-minute 10-K again and stopped thinking about marathons altogether. I didn't even make it to the '88 Olympic trials."

But he stubbornly refused to stop running, because running was how Salazar defined himself. Running was the means by which he proved his manhood. At the age that Alberto was now, his father had already fought in the Sierra Maestra against Batista. Jose Salazar had steadfastly followed his friend and comrade Fidel Castro until Castro assumed power and aligned with the Communists. Then

Fidel told Jose, who now designed tourist facilities for the revolutionary government, that he couldn't build a church because there was no room for God in the revolution—just build hotels. His father told Fidel, in so many words, to take his hotels and shove them up his Marxist-Leninist butt.

He flew to Miami just a few minutes ahead of Castro's agents with just a single suitcase and a few hundred dollars to his name. He trained in the Everglades for the Bay of Pigs invasion, but didn't go to Cuba because he was convinced that the CIA and Kennedy were a bunch of fools, liars, and cowards, too weak and timid to fully support the mission. Castro crushed the invasion before it was Jose's turn to embark. So the Cuban exiles, the men of valor, were forced to spend the rest of their lives preparing for the next invasion. Jose lived by that obligation while at the same time becoming a success as an American civil engineer, building a new life on sheer roaring will, imbuing that will in his sons, who must be true and strong and never back down. And in the marathon, Alberto had discovered the perfect vehicle to please and fulfill his father.

But now the marathon had deserted him. Alberto was just another ex-jock sitting in a cocktail lounge with a stack of menus under his arm. So what if he owned the restaurant? What kind of work was this for a man of valor? Running was his destiny. A man pursued his destiny with single-minded devotion. Alberto's favorite movie was *Raging Bull*. He thought it was the greatest movie ever made. He saw the film again and again, identifying with Jake La Motta's rage and obsession. But remember what happened to Jake La Motta when he was through as a prizefighter? He turned into a monster, a clown, a parody of his true self. The same thing was now happening to Alberto, although he took pains to hide it from the world.

Not even Molly knew the depth of his sadness. A man did not show weakness. Alberto fulfilled his duties. He operated his restaurant with a streak of iron, instilling fear and respect in his often feckless young staff. He smiled for the fans who asked to have their photos taken with him. He coached his son's soccer team. During University of Oregon track meets, he sat in the Hayward stands next to Bowerman and Phil Knight. He heard the respectful whispers when he passed: Look, there goes Salazar. Alberto moved through life and only he knew he was sleepwalking.

Everything had become a chore, a problem, an effort. The world had turned gray. Why couldn't he run? Why couldn't he sleep? Why couldn't he feel anything? At odd moments during the day—driving his car or in the dead afternoon hours at the restaurant, quiet in the place, only the vacuum humming—Alberto would stare out the window, thinking that he didn't really want to die. But if some accident were to occur—if he should somehow smash his car into a wall up in the hills above Hayward Field like Prefontaine, or if the kind of disaster that had recently befallen Beardsley should visit him—well, if that happened, it might not be such a terrible thing.

He couldn't run, yet he couldn't stop running. Salazar reached the point where the best he could do was cover 4 or 5 miles in a crabbed shuffle.

"For much of the last 10 years, I hated running," he confessed to a reporter in 1994. "I hated it with a passion. I used to wish for a cataclysmic injury in which I would lose one of my legs. I know that sounds terrible, but if I had lost a leg, then I wouldn't have to torture myself anymore."

8

With each mile past Wellesley, another runner dropped off the lead pack. The air temperature had lifted into the low 70s, and the sun heated the pavement to more than 90 degrees. Bill Rodgers continued to run strongly, surging to the lead for a mile, and it briefly seemed that he might summon a ghost-dance effort and contend for the victory. At mile 16, however, just before the firehouse at the base of the Braeburn Hill, Rodgers faded. Just beyond the firehouse, Ed Mendoza, who'd been looking fresh up to that point, abruptly dropped away. Now it was down to Beardsley and Salazar. Beardsley stepped to the lead he would hold for the next 9 miles.

Despite the fact that this was his first Boston Marathon, Dick felt remarkably comfortable. His race was proceeding according to plan. Unlike Salazar, however, he was not at all certain that his plan would yield victory. He could run the race of his dreams and still lose to Alberto by a quarter mile. Indeed, his one-step "lead" was barely a lead at all; hanging just off Beardsley's left shoulder, Salazar shared control of the race. All Beardsley could do was savor the fact that no other runner had been able to hang with Salazar so far into a marathon. The heat worked to Dick's advantage. Any challenge or obstacle—heat, cold, wind, hills, rain, snow, ice, any factor that made a marathon more difficult, that sapped Salazar's energy and neutralized, however slightly, his superior closing speed—worked to Beardsley's advantage.

The soles of his racing flats flicked over the hot asphalt. The towns—Wellesley, Needham, Natick—passed in a welter of color, bleats of plastic horns like you heard in the ballparks, spectators clapping and cupping their hands to their mouths to shout incomprehensible words of encouragement, little kids and the occasional full-grown bozo running alongside for 10 yards so they could say they knew what leading the Boston Marathon felt like, people holding up signs, acrid wafts of cigarette and marijuana smoke, boom boxes blaring Springsteen's *Born to Run* and the theme from *Chariots of Fire,* and over it all, poured like spun honey, the effulgent spring sunshine.

Ten paces ahead—always 10 paces ahead, the distance never varying, creating an unpleasant, Pavlovian, mouse-on-a-treadmill effect—the pace truck with its digital clock read out the time elapsed since the start in Hopkinton. Ahead of the pace truck lurked the big flatbed press truck with its important jut of cameras. The reporters stood on the truck bed behind the photographers, fighting to maintain their balance through the truck's fits and starts.

Dick ran in a flowing violent rhythm, the efficient explosions of his lungs like the long humming explosion maintained by a finely tuned automobile engine. On the run, Beardsley felt most like himself, yet not like himself at all. Avid and sentient, remorseless and impersonal. There was nobody else to make happy, nothing to fulfill but his own nature. It was almost as if he were back in high school again, running the gravel roads around Wayzata with his best friend, George Ross.

"We got into some pretty good battles," Dick recalled in his autobiography. "On an 8- or 10-mile run, we didn't say boo to each other for about the last 5 because we were trying to drive each other into the ground. The minute we'd finish, we were best friends again, but those last 5 miles we tried to bury each other. Coming down the final half-mile stretch—they lived on a gravel road, and as you got closer to their house, it was a gradual down-hill—we just flew. We flew down that hill."

Now, battling through the mid-reaches of the Boston Marathon next to Salazar, Beardsley continually monitored his physical systems: the beat of his pulse, the swing of his hips, the clean chuff of his breath like the sound of a child sleeping. He inventoried his pain. Running at this speed, you could fly apart at any moment. All it took was one foot-plant a centimeter awry, a single offer of water declined.

Since he'd slipped on the ice while training a few years ago, Beardsley's right knee had been suspect. All runners, however, had their own version of that knee, their own particular trouble. Most aches healed, but there was always one that you carried from town to town, race to race, year to year, that you just hoped and prayed and worked desperately to conceal. You couldn't let your opponent see it; insofar as possible, you denied it to yourself. Even Salazar had something to hide.

They ran down the gentle decline from Wellesley Square to Lower Newton Falls. As the gulf widened between Salazar and Beardsley and the rest of the field, the pitch of the crowd noise altered. The spectators' attention quickened; they grew less frivolous. The two runners sensed the change and moved more intently, holding their pace as they appraised one another. It was as if they were formally meeting for the first time.

Dick could hear Alberto's wheels turning. During some stretches, for as long as a quarter mile or half mile at a time, he felt as if he were connected to Salazar; it was hard to tell where he ended and Alberto began. That was cool, he thought, and that was frightening. The pain had begun. By the end of the hills, he realized, the pain would surpass any he'd yet encountered in a marathon. He didn't know if he'd win, but he knew he was running better than he ever had before. The hills waited a few miles ahead.

The sun was behind them, so Beardsley could watch Salazar's shadow on the pavement. When the shadow began to move forward, Dick speeded up just enough to stay ahead of it. From this point forward, he could not afford to let Salazar take the lead.

9

n July 1995, Dick Beardsley's father lay dying from pancreatic cancer. Dick's sister Maryann called from Michigan, where Bill Beardsley was receiving hospice care, to say that the end was near—72 hours, at most. If Dick wanted to see his father again, he should come immediately. Dick discussed the situation with Mary. They decided that she and their son, Andy, whom they had adopted as an infant in Honduras in 1986, would stay in Minnesota, then come for the funeral. Dick would start driving to Michigan the next morning.

While preparing for the journey, his first thought wasn't about his father, or about his wife or child, or even about readying his pickup truck; Dick's first concern was pills. He didn't have enough to last a week, which was the minimum amount of time he'd likely spend in Michigan. In fact, at the rate he'd been gobbling them, he doubted whether he'd have enough for a normal weekend at home—or what recently passed for normal. It was Thursday afternoon, moreover, when doctors often left their offices to get an early start on a long summer weekend. This could be a problem. No, this was a problem. He would have to go to Fargo immediately to secure more pain pills.

Fargo, North Dakota, lay 40 miles west of Detroit Lakes, Minnesota, where Dick and his family had lived for the past year. Their time in the town had been the happiest—or, more accurately, the least miserable—since his farm accident in November of '89. Beardsley's healing process had been arduous, with a seemingly endless series of complications and setbacks. For starters, at the time of the PTO accident, the family lacked health insurance. That distressing situation, like many others over the last 6 years, had been Dick's fault. He had known that his health coverage had lapsed; he was meaning to purchase a new policy, but he kept putting it off. Providentially, the national running community learned of his predicament and raised thousands of dollars to help cover Beardsley's medical expenses. The money eased his debt but added to his sense of guilt.

"At night, I had terrible nightmares," he would remember about his first stay in the hospital after the accident. "Always, always I saw the power takeoff, except now it was Mary or Andy caught in it. I'd wake up from the nightmares sweating so much my bedclothes would be soaked. There were many nights when a nurse sat next to my bed, holding my hand until I fell asleep."

There was plenty to feel guilty about. He had dragged Mary out to the farm. Then after just a few months, he'd carelessly suffered a near-fatal injury that forced Mary to do all the farmwork, take care of little Andy, and, when Dick finally came home from the hospital after multiple surgeries, take care of him as well. He worked furiously on rehab, lifting weights to strengthen his leg with the obsession he once poured into running and the farm. He grew stronger but then developed an infection that sent him back to the hospital.

Beardsley spent large chunks of the next several years in hospitals. In July of '92, Mary, Andy, and Dick were driving home from a visit to Wisconsin. As they passed through an intersection, another driver ran a stop sign. Swerving to avoid the vehicle, Dick ran his pickup truck into a ditch. Mary and Andy were unhurt, but Dick suffered neck and back injuries. As the paramedics loaded him into the ambulance, Dick's thoughts turned black: He was all busted up again. "A lady runs a stop sign, and life is chaos once more," he thought. But then he brightened—at the hospital, maybe he'd get a little more of that Demerol.

By the following winter, Beardsley was strong enough to resume limited running. One snowy day, while out for a run, he was struck by a hit-and-run driver. At the hospital, his pain was treated with Demerol and Percocet. Back home after his release, he fainted and fell down a flight of stairs, which earned him yet another trip to the hospital. There he was given a push-button pump with which he could self-administer Demerol. Dick rode the pump as hard as his father used to clutch his gin bottle.

He was discharged from the hospital. A few weeks later, in another snowstorm, he was driving home from a speaking engagement in the Twin Cities. Beardsley spun off the road, crashed, and spent another week in the hospital with head and back injuries. He was given more painkillers. Back home, he went out for a run and felt a stabbing pain in his back. Doctors prescribed Percocet.

Years later, while giving an anti-drug-abuse talk at an elementary school, Beardsley recited this biblical litany of affliction. A boy raised his hand. "Mr. Beardsley, don't you think you were having all these accidents on purpose so you could get more drugs?"

Until that boy made the seemingly obvious connection, Beardsley says, he had been blind to it.

In the spring of 1994, he underwent a series of back and knee surgeries that generated the now-familiar cycle of pain and medication. The following year, a fishing guide business came up for sale in Detroit Lakes, a town in western Minnesota near the North

Dakota line, the area where Dick's father took him fishing when he was a boy. Beardsley loved angling almost as much as he did running or farming. He possessed the affinity and sociability that serve a fishing guide so well. Most important, Dick and his family needed a change of scenery and a fresh start. So he bought the guide business and the bait shop that went with it. In most ways, the move proved fortuitous. The business prospered, and his family loved the friendly town of 8,000, which boasted 500 lakes within a 20-mile radius. If things were finally looking up for Beardsley, however, they weren't looking completely new. He located a couple of physicians whom he could readily work for pain pills. They practiced in the Fargo metropolitan area.

Beardsley set out for Fargo late on that July afternoon, passing the southwest shore of Detroit Lake, named in the early 1800s by a pioneer Jesuit priest as he sought to save Chippewa souls and plant the French flag in the new world. For the previous few centuries, the only white people venturing into this territory had been fur trappers. The country was densely forested and dotted with thousands of lakes, the detritus of the Ice Age. The glaciers had receded from northern Minnesota just 10,000 years before, on the edge of human consciousness and history. Archetypal remnants from that era lingered to the present: the moose and the wolf, the Chippewa reservation running from just north of town to near the Canadian border. Subzero temperatures were the rule from Thanksgiving through St. Patrick's Day. The summers were hot and muggy and so mosquito- and black-fly-infested that Beardsley would not run in the woods from early May until November's first hard frost.

Now the lake glittered in the summer sunshine. The previous September, the inaugural Dick Beardsley Half-Marathon had looped around Detroit Lake. Beardsley presided over the highly successful race while zonked to the gills on Demerol. But nobody in town harbored suspicions. Beardsley, for his part, had convinced himself that he wasn't really hooked. He felt great, and his guide business was booming. The key to the enterprise wasn't catching fish so much as entertaining a client, making him feel comfortable. Occasionally a client would request, before or after time on the water, to run a few miles with the man who'd engaged in the famous Duel in the Sun with Alberto Salazar. Dick always obliged. The client would be thrilled. If Beardsley were truly hooked, he wouldn't have been able to pull that off, would he?

No, he told himself, he wasn't an addict. He just needed a little bit of the edge taken off. Besides, he had endured a truckload of pain, physical and otherwise. And now his father was dying.

Dick put the visor down against the westering sun. Over all, the news was a blessing. His father had suffered greatly from his illness. He had taken cancer head-on, just like he'd finally confronted his alcoholism. Bill Beardsley had been sober for the last 13 years. A few weeks after the 1982 Boston Marathon, he had knocked back a final martini, then gone stone-dry. No AA, no medications, just plain no. He hadn't touched a drop, not even after he was laid off from his sales job, after he split up with Dick's mother, or after he was diagnosed with terminal cancer 8 months ago and it didn't matter anymore how much he drank. During these years, with the drunkenness no longer between them, Bill and Dick had grown very close. Now, ironically, the monkey rode on the son's back instead of the father's.

Dick had a headache. Well, not really a headache, more like a faint uneasiness roiling every nerve in his body. Dad was dying. Well, okay, he would work on that later. There would be plenty of time to think during tomorrow's trip. Right now he had to get pills or there wouldn't be a trip.

The drive to Fargo was flat and featureless. Beardsley barely registered the passing lakes, farms, and towns. Nothing else mattered but acquiring opioids. What Dick liked best was coming home after a sunny day on the lake when the walleye had been biting and his clients hadn't been jerks. Wash out the boat, untangle the lines, rig the reels for tomorrow's clients. Answer the phone calls and other messages that had piled up during the day, each one a prospective client or request to speak. Over the last several years, Beardsley had become a popular motivational speaker for youth and business groups. People enjoyed hearing his stories, especially the one about running against Salazar at the '82 Boston Marathon.

After he finished his end-of-the-day chores, Dick would duck into the bathroom or out to the garage to the cab of his pickup. He would pop a couple Demerol—tossing them into his mouth as if they were M&M's or sunflower seeds—and gulp the pills down dry, then settle into his easy chair. He'd snap on the TV, open a magazine, wait for a minute, then feel that flow and ease, that inward flowering, that fist unclenching. Dick would hear a bluebird singing just for him.

That was Beardsley's ideal way to get loaded. But right now, he was just thinking maintenance dose. It was 4:30 already, and the traffic was thick on Highway 10. The afternoon heat lay heavy on the meadows of the roadside farms. The insects chanted and buzzed loudly.

He was driving hard to get to a doctor's office in Fargo. He needed a new doctor even though Kennedy was closer. In fact, he was passing Dr. Kennedy's clinic right now, tucked into a big-box shopping mall on the outskirts of Moorhead, Minnesota, which was just across the Red River and state line from Fargo. For his first 6 months in Detroit Lakes, Beardsley had gotten his pills from

Kennedy's back clinic. But the physician eventually grew wary of Beardsley's consumption and cut off the supply.

Nope, sorry, Dick. I can't give you any more pills. You know, you might think about weaning yourself off of that stuff. If you need help . . .

So now Dick had to go across the river into North Dakota to see this doctor, an orthopedic surgeon. This doctor would certainly help him out. It might take some doing, however. Dick might have to go into his limping, crippled, death's-door routine. Over the last year or so, he'd become an accomplished actor. He had learned to twist his shoulders, neck, and back into a cramped, rigor mortis–like position that actually did invoke considerable pain. So when he hobbled into the doctor's office, ashen-faced and grimacing, the receptionist would jump up, rush over, help him into a wheelchair, and roll him straight in to see the doctor, who was only human after all, who could recognize true suffering and do his best to alleviate it. The doc would write a prescription. If the pain was real, and the doc wrote the slip, then it was all legitimate, right? So what was the problem?

Beardsley worked through the dense rush-hour bridge traffic, growing increasingly frantic as five o'clock neared. *Can you believe this lady what'd she do fall asleep move it lady move it move it please.* Finally, he pulled into the medical center. He sprinted across the parking lot, then slowed to a halting limp as he entered the doctor's office and greeted the receptionist.

"Hey, Janice, how are ya?"

"Hey, Dick. Just fine, thanks. But oh my, you don't look so swell."

"Yeah, well. This darn back, Janice. Listen, I was wondering if the doctor might be able to squeeze me in. I have to drive to Michigan tomorrow. My dad's not doing real good."

"Oh, Dick, I'm so sorry to hear that, but I'm afraid the doctor is already gone for the day. But listen, I can move some people around, get you in first thing Monday morning or anytime next week."

"No, thanks, Janice, that's okay. I was just taking a shot."

"You sure, Dick?"

"Yeah, I'm sure. Hey, no problem."

"Well, all right then. Have a nice weekend, Dick."

"You too, Janice."

Beardsley walked back out to the pickup. *Shit damn what do I do now?*

He drove back across the Red River bridge with the sun setting big and red in his rearview mirror. The traffic was still heavy, citizens moving eagerly into their summer evening. How can they do it straight? Dick wondered. How can they make it without a little help? Why would they even want to?

Beardsley was unlikely to be the only strung-out driver crossing the Red River bridge that afternoon. Millions of Americans abused prescription drugs. So maybe that guy on his Harley was one of Dick's clan, or that pretty girl in the Corolla, or maybe even that mom with her kids, driving the minivan home. Anything was possible, but at the same time nothing mattered other than the fact that Beardsley was driving 400 miles tomorrow morning and his pill box had only three units rattling around in it.

He already knew what he was going to do, but it was too difficult to articulate, even to himself. Almost by its own volition, the Chevy pickup with Dick Beardsley Fishing emblazoned across it worked its way through Moorhead on Route 10, continuing to the eastern edge of town and the shopping mall where Dr. Kennedy's back clinic occupied a storefront office between a giant Kmart and an equally mammoth Target. The clinic would be closed by now, but Beardsley had business elsewhere in the mall. He parked a good distance from the Kmart, but not so far as to arouse suspicion.

Dick reached in the back of the cab, rummaged around, found the cardboard accordion briefcase, and very carefully extracted a 5-by-7 slip of paper. A month or so ago, the doctor had referred Beardsley to a massage therapist in Detroit Lakes. The orthopedist had jotted the phone number on a leaf from his personalized prescription pad. It would be a simple matter to white-out the number, make a copy of the altered page, and forge a prescription on it with the doctor's signature. Beardsley studied the piece of paper; other than the small, neatly written phone number, it was immaculate. What could this be but an invitation—a veritable command—to do for himself what the doctor certainly would have done for him, had he been in his office?

Beardsley started the truck and drove across the highway to the Kinko's copy center that he'd seen a hundred times on his trips to Moorhead and Fargo. This was another sign—if Dick wasn't meant to deal with this problem himself, then God wouldn't have made the solution so convenient. Dick was a great believer in signs and omens. Back in June 1981, for example, he was driving to Duluth to run Grandma's Marathon, his breakthrough race, in which he went from solid pro to the world-class ranks. Squires and Beardsley both thought he was capable of a 2:09 performance but weren't inviting a jinx by talking about it, even to one another. Driving north on I-35 from the Twin Cities, the first mile marker Beardsley saw was a 209. In Duluth, his hotel room was 902—2:09 backwards. He had gone on to log his 2:09:36 victory, setting the stage for the Duel in the Sun 9 months later in Boston.

Well, Beardsley thought, with the cracked logic of an addict, wasn't the presence of this Kinko's another sign? Wasn't fate communing with him again?

Using glue and an X-Acto knife, he carefully eclipsed the phone number with a sliver of white paper. Inside Kinko's, he ran off a dozen copies—what the heck, better make it two dozen—of the doctored prescription slips. They came out crisp, clean, and indistinguishable from the original. Or were they? He held the copies up to the light, looking for watermarks. There were probably a dozen hidden defenses that the system had installed to prevent forgeries. He was going to get caught for sure. But darned if he could see any difference between the copies and the original, and he doubted if a busy pharmacist would find any either. Stay positive, Dick told himself. Besides, qualms or quibbles were nothing in the face of his need.

He drove back across the highway to the same parking space outside the Kmart, at whose pharmacy he frequently filled his pain-pill prescriptions. He took out his pen and the stack of altered prescription slips and set to work. For years now, he'd been reading prescriptions, so it wasn't too difficult to affect a doc's hasty scrawl and terse pharmaceutical shorthand; such dry terms, he thought, for such a glorious medicine. Surprisingly quickly, Beardsley produced a good copy of the doctor's hand. In fact, an excellent copy. For a few moments, he sat appraising his work with a mixture of pride and horror. For his whole life, he'd thought of himself as one person, when he was really somebody else.

Beardsley's friends had told him about experiencing similar moments: the first time they'd shoplifted a candy bar, cut school, or cheated on their wives. Sitting in the hot sun in the Kmart parking lot, with people and cars passing all around on everyday errands, Dick realized that what he was about to do ran counter to all of his training and beliefs, to the most basic and reassuring image he'd constructed of the world and his role and identity in it. Unlike his friends, he had never shoplifted a candy bar, cut school, or cheated on his wife. (Although he had the chance at the London Marathon back in '81. The race director had provided "escorts" for the elite runners, and Dick had had this shimmery taffeta-clad number slithering against him all through the awards ceremony. All he had to do was take her up to his room. But he was not about to break his vow to Mary. The flash of friction, he knew, would only yield endless remorse.) He had never taken a single shortcut during his running career. He had never doped and never backed down from a challenge, not even from Alberto Salazar over the last miles at Boston when the pain got so bad it was beyond pain.

In the rapidly fading light of his innocence and inexperience, moreover, Beardsley was sure he'd get caught, and in the most glaring and ignominious manner. He envisioned handcuffs and a crowd of scandalized bystanders watching the fourth-fastest American marathoner of all time getting shoved into the back of a squad car. This was his chance to save himself, he realized; rip up the forgery, drive straight to a hospital emergency room, and plead for help. He also fantasized this scene—his tears, Mary's tears, reassuring hands on his shoulder, then flashing ahead to a bright afternoon in the indeterminate future, Dick clipping a life vest snugly around a beaming Andy, starting the outboard motor, then gliding into a blue lake and waving to Mary, who stood on the dock blowing kisses to her brave and sober husband.

Beardsley let this image kindle, glow, then finally fade. He climbed out of his truck and walked across the Kmart parking lot to begin his life of crime.

Alberto Salazar and his father in 1979, after Alberto had won the Freedom Trail road race in Boston

Dick Beardsley on his father's shoulders in 1957

Dick Beardsley on the farm in Minnesota, 1982

Left to Right: Beardsley, Bill Rodgers, Salazar, Ed Mendoza, near the midpoint of the '82 Boston Marathon. Rodgers and Mendoza would soon fade.

Jose Salazar (front row center, kneeling) training for the Bay of Pigs invasion in the Florida Everglades, December 1960. On April 17, 1961, the day of the invasion, this group of men stood in reserve at an airstrip in Nicaragua but did not embark for Cuba.

Beardsley and Salazar pass Coolidge Corner in Brookline, near the 23-mile mark.

At Kenmore Square, near Fenway Park, Beardsley and Salazar enter the marathon's final mile. There were no sidewalk barriers; spectators pressed as close as they wanted to the runners.

Dick Beardsley in Detroit Lakes, Minnesota, January 2004

Alberto Salazar in Beaverton, Oregon, January 2004

Salazar and Beardsley, steps away from the finish line

Dick Beardsley and Alberto Salazar together in Detroit Lakes, Minnesota, September 2003

Moments after the finish in downtown Boston. Salazar was later taken to the medical tent, where he received fluids intravenously. The morning after the marathon, Beardsley went out for a jog.

10

After watching the early part of the race on television and discovering that an extraordinary contest was in progress—two runners, stripped down to bone and will, relentlessly moving down the streets of their city—the citizens of the Boston area turned out of their houses to witness the final miles. Fathers lifted their children up on their shoulders and told them to pay attention. An estimated crowd of two million turned out to watch some part of the 1982 Boston Marathon.

Meanwhile, on the other side of the world, Lt. Ricardo Salazar sailed the Indian Ocean aboard the aircraft carrier *John F. Kennedy*. An F-14 fighter pilot, Ricardo had just repaired to his stateroom for the evening. It was past 10:00 p.m. at that longitude, and he was ready to turn in.

"I was vaguely aware that it was Patriots' Day back in Massachusetts and that Alberto was running the Boston Marathon," Ricardo remembered. "But to be honest, when you're on sea duty, life back stateside tends to get pretty distant and abstract. Remember, this was more than 20 years ago, and we didn't have e-mail and satellite TV and all the other communications that we've got now. I wasn't really tuned in to what was happening in the marathon."

A great deal was happening, both in the front of the race, where

Ricardo's brother, Alberto, and Dick Beardsley were nearing the Newton Hills, and in the ranks, where more than 6,000 other runners were embarked on their own pilgrimages. One was John Lodwick, who would finish third in the race. Like Salazar, Lodwick was a member of Nike's elite Eugene-based Athletics West team. Unlike Salazar, Lodwick, whose 2:10:52 personal-best time still ranks among the 30 fastest marathons ever run by an American, earned a sustenance-level annual stipend of around $15,000. He did not think he was underpaid.

"It was a tremendous amount of work and a tremendous amount of fun," Lodwick says of his years as a professional runner. "All of us in AW were good friends. With the exception of Alberto and one or two others, nobody was making a lot of money. But it didn't matter. We were young and single and caught up in something important—something that was much more than a sport. I was extremely serious about running, obviously, but I primarily thought of it as a way to know and serve God. For me, running was a way to witness. At times, at its best, running could even be a form of prayer."

Lodwick, who now serves as the pastor of Eastmont Baptist Church in Bend, Oregon, ran seven Boston Marathons, logging several top-10 finishes. He took a conservative tack in the '82 race, running the second half of the marathon faster than the first.

"I remember Beardsley, Salazar, Rodgers, and Mendoza breaking away from the pack at Wellesley and moving so far ahead they seemed to be running a separate race," Lodwick says. "Over the second half, I picked up my pace and started passing people. As I approached Heartbreak Hill at mile 21, I could see Bill Rodgers ahead. Bill was really struggling at that point—as I went past him, I touched his shoulder in respect.

"The crowds were huge. You could barely even tell that there was a hill there because of all the people. And the noise! At first I couldn't figure it out. Then I realized that a very long time must have passed since Alberto and Dick had gone by. The crowd was so hungry to see another runner—they were so pumped up by the duel between the two leaders—that they went nuts when I came along. Even today, 21 years later, I still get chills when I remember that roar. It echoed and reverberated into this deafening, almost palpable wall of sound. It was very powerful. It sounded almost holy."

Other runners took a more secular but no less soulful approach to the marathon. "Challenge the Boston and you must be at your peak," warned Dr. George Sheehan, the sage of the running boom. "Accept your limitation and, with care, the thinking runner will have a comfortable, creditable race. But go for broke and prepare to be broken."

One of the citizen-runners going for broke that day was a 38-year-old attorney named David Hobler, who was running his first Boston Marathon. In the mid-1960s, fresh out of Stanford University Law School, Hobler had helped spring Ken Kesey from jail after one of the countercultural novelist's pot busts. Hobler later had moved to Hawaii to work legal aid, surf the Pipeline break at Enukai Beach and partake of the fruit of those heady times. Tripping on mescaline, he would watch the sun rise over Diamond Head. One Sunday morning, coming down from mescaline, he happened across a training run for the Honolulu Marathon. He met an army colonel who was running 14 miles and a ponytailed glassblower who was running 16. Hobler, fascinated, took up the pursuit himself, becoming a fixture in the Hawaiian running community.

"Running was a practical and a mystical discipline," he says. "It was a way of melding the inner and outer realms. As a runner, you could compete and excel—you could calibrate just about every step that you took. Or you could throw away the damn watch, forget about competition, and use running to blow yourself out of your gourd."

Indeed, Hobler—now clean and sober and the founder of the seminal 12-step group Runners in Recovery—remembers the 1982 Boston Marathon in terms strikingly similar to Lodwick's. "I felt like I could see and hear everything," he recalls. "When I crossed the finish line that afternoon, I felt glorious, like I was going to live forever."

Hobler finished the marathon in 3:04, near the middle of the pack. He was one of the thousands of citizen-runners who trained almost as many miles and endured nearly as much pain as Beardsley or Salazar. Yet they had no professional stake and pursued no tangible reward other than a bowl of beef stew, the Boston Marathon's traditional postrace refreshment.

"If you talk to an elite or near-elite American distance runner today, they'll tell you that the primary aim of their training is to avoid injury," says Tom Derderian, a former member and current coach of the Greater Boston Track Club and the author of a history of the Boston Marathon. "If you had talked to a similar athlete 25 years ago—somebody doing the '82 Boston, for example—he would have told you the idea of training was to run fast."

Derderian thinks that his baby-boom generation of American distance runners excelled because they approached the sport with single-minded, starving-artist-like devotion. "We didn't have a whole lot going on in our lives besides running," he points out. "No cell phones or e-mail, no PhD programs, no flights to Aruba for spring break." He also cites the fact that serious distance runners of the era banded together in tightly knit communities, in which peer pressure and intramural competition led to continuous improvement. Baby boomers were drawn to the sport, Derderian theorizes, due to a singular convergence of historical forces.

"Baby boomers in general and boomer distance runners in particular were heirs both to the warrior mentality of their World War II–veteran fathers and the new consciousness of the 1960s and '70s," he explains. "Both ways of thinking were essentially idealistic and challenged us to adopt causes greater than ourselves. The marathon served as an ideal outlet for both types of energy. Running a fast marathon was difficult. It required enormous discipline, willpower, and competitive drive—the influences of our warrior fathers. On the other hand, marathoning was an elemental, nonexploitative, natural form of personal expression—the spirit of the counterculture. I think that the majority of the runners toeing the line at Boston in '82, either consciously or unconsciously, were riding that double wave."

Bill Squires watched the race on a TV monitor above the finish line while providing color commentary for a local station's marathon telecast. The gig was proving less than a smash hit. No one knew more about the Boston Marathon than Squires, but no one was less capable of condensing his knowledge into a sound bite. "Now look, what I told Dickie to do here is wait and sit on Al's shoulder, but he decided to take the lead instead," Squires tried to explain to his announcer partner. "Which isn't really so different from what I told him. Because Al is pushing the pace, too, you see. Just because Al's not leading doesn't necessarily mean he's behind. My little disciple has listened well. Because, you see, running uphill actually forces you to take shorter steps and relax the muscles . . . "

The announcer gave Squires an uncomprehending stare. The

third announcer stepped in. "Didn't you coach Salazar at one point, Bill?"

"Sure. Al came to me when he was a 16-year-old. You shoulda seen this kid . . . "

"So, any divided loyalties on your part?"

"Now? Nah. We work for different people. Al's a Nike athlete. I'm a consultant for the New Balance track club. That's who Dickie runs for. A few days ago, I ran into Al and his dad when they were at the . . . "

"So can you tell us what's going through Salazar's mind right now?"

Squires paused. Al would be thinking that Dickie was tough, much tougher than he expected. But Al would also be thinking that he still had this race in the bag. Because he had the kick. Because he was Alberto Salazar.

"Well," Squires told the announcer, "he's thinking that the hills are coming. The real race is getting ready to start."

As Al and Dickie entered the hills, Squires tried to explain that the race wasn't really the way it looked on TV. On the TV screen, it looked like the two guys were running steady and regular and even-paced. You would never know that they were surging and feinting and making moves and changing up the rhythm like a good pitcher in baseball keeps changing speeds on the batter. Dickie was charging hard then backing off, surging and slowing for different distances each time, trying to confuse Alberto, open just the slightest wedge of daylight, put the slightest shadow of doubt into Al's mind. Dickie was throwing the kitchen sink at Al. But there was no way to explain that to these birds or to the boys and girls out there in TV land.

In the increasingly long gaps between his "commentary," Squires thought about the marathon. He took all his runners out on the Boston course to learn its angles and grades and the taste of the air and even the smell of the fry-grease blowing out from the grills in the Natick grinder joints. He would have his athletes run up and down Heartbreak so often that they saw it in their dreams. He would take a tennis ball and roll it down Commonwealth Avenue so his runners would know what line to follow. He told his guys how to save a few steps by running close to the curb. Hold back here, cut loose there, he advised them. Above all, never ever run at a steady pace. Don't let the other guy figure you out. Always keep him guessing.

"I taught my guys to constantly change their move patterns," Squires says. "For instance, the natural tendency of a runner is to rest once he climbs to the top of a hill. My athletes would get to the top of a hill, fake like they were going to lay down and die, and then take off. It would catch the other guy with his thumb up his butt."

Squires's ideal runner wasn't the fastest or the most talented. Any fool with a clipboard and whistle could coach a thoroughbred, he often said. What Squires sought was a smart, tough runner who would listen, who understood that the marathon was like a chess match. Knocking out the other guy's queen with showy moves was well and good, but usually the guy who had the most pawns won.

The coach arrived at his textured, tactical understanding of the Boston Marathon by a route at once direct and circular. As a boy growing up in Arlington, Massachusetts, he breathed in stories of New England's rich sporting traditions like oxygen. He dreamed of becoming a star running back, but he was too small and thin for football. So, like countless scrawny athletes before him, Squires gravitated to track and field, developing into an outstanding middle-distance runner. At the University of Notre Dame, he was a four-time

All-American with a 4:06 personal best for the mile. After graduating, he returned to the Boston area to teach and coach at Wakefield High School. He continued his running career on the winter indoor track circuit, which, in the late 1950s, was still thriving in towns and cities throughout New England and the Northeast.

Due to the rather Draconian rules of the time, however, Squires couldn't retain his amateur status while getting paid to coach. When a local Amateur Athletic Union official told Squires he had to turn in his competitor's card, Squires asked to be allowed to enter one final race: the 1960 Boston Marathon, which was just a few months away. The official agreed. Squires trained furiously, doubling his weekly training mileage, assiduously running the Newton Hills. On Patriots' Day, Squires finished 20th in 2:47:46. "That race was very important to me," he told author Hal Higdon. "It provided a mental perspective for teaching others how to run well at Boston."

That perspective delivered a canny, gritty, middle-distance runner's approach to the marathon. By Squires's lights, a marathoner didn't cruise, he competed. At the same time, a runner shouldn't be intimidated by the marathon. He could play with the distance, provided that he first submitted to the punishing levels of preparation that playfulness required.

"Squires said the more you can get your body used to accelerating, then backing off, then flying up and down hills, then recovering, then sprinting—the more you do this kind of thing in practice, the more ready you are when you get in a race," Beardsley recalled in his autobiography. "I learned quickly that if I had to talk to Coach on the phone, I'd better do it early in the day. If I talked to him at, say, eight o'clock at night, I couldn't get to sleep. I wanted to run the workout right then. He got me so fired up I'd just lie in bed feeling the adrenaline pound its way through my body."

Despite their gaping differences in age and background, the match between the middle-aged big-city coach and the young country-bred Beardsley seemed to be one struck in heaven. Both were incorrigibly garrulous; possessed an infectious, if often cornball, sense of humor; and were intensely loyal and emotional. Both were passionately committed to distance running, and both masked a keen intelligence behind a bumptious facade. The timing of the two men's meeting, moreover, had been fortuitous. Squires assumed Beardsley's reins when the latter was physically mature and nearing the peak of his marathoning career. The coach provided just the right tactical and motivational patina to bring Beardsley's running to full luster.

Squires's relationship with Salazar, by contrast, was based on almost the exact opposite set of circumstances. About all that he and Alberto shared were the same hometown and an obsession with the marathon. In personality and temperament, the two were polar opposites. Salazar, moreover, fell under the coach's influence at the dawn of his running career. Rather than provide a finishing sheen, Squires applied Alberto's underlying primer. This was largely a matter of holding the young runner back. Alberto recognized his destiny from the time he was 16 years old; Squires's task was to keep him from pursuing it too soon. Wait to run the marathon, he told the rookie again and again; wait until you are ready.

Several years after Salazar left Boston, when he was at the pinnacle of his career, he and Squires met at a track meet in Oslo, Norway. Salazar went for a run through the trails of a city park, and Squires accompanied him. At the park, they met Henry Rono, who was also competing at the Oslo meet. The three men chatted for a few minutes, then Rono and Salazar took off on their respective workouts. Squires ambled down a trail. He had gone just a short distance when Rono ran back to him and stopped.

"Henry looked me in the eye and made this very solemn kind of pronouncement: 'Out of all the runners I have competed against, Salazar is the bravest,'" Squires recalled. "Then he took off again. It was vintage Henry—a little weird, but very impressive, too. Henry wanted to tell me what he thought about Al in private. He didn't want Alberto around to hear."

And now, as the 1982 Boston Marathon pounded toward its climax, Bill Squires realized that, of all the marathoners he had coached over the years, only three truly understood his idiosyncratic, inspired approach to the event. One of them was Bill Rodgers. The other two ran in each other's shadow, desperately trying to break one another, as if their lives depended on the outcome.

Heartbreak Hill consists of a long, gradual climb up a commercial strip of Commonwealth Avenue through the suburban town of Newton at the Boston Marathon's 21-mile mark. The culminating hill in a succession of four progressively higher ones, Heartbreak lifts about 80 feet over the distance of a mile. Had it not been so memorably named by sportswriter Jerry Nason of the *Boston Globe,* it might be regarded as just another difficult stretch of an exceedingly difficult course.

In the 1936 race, Tarzan Brown (a member of New England's Narragansett Indian tribe and a two-time Boston winner) had been struggling to maintain his lead when he reached the hill. Johnny Kelley, who'd been running in second place, pulled up to Brown, gave him a pat on the shoulder, then steamed into the lead. In the ensuing miles, however, Brown rallied to victory while Kelley faded to a fifth-place finish. Nason described Kelley as "losing the race on Heartbreak Hill." The name stuck. In 1979, Joan Benoit Samuelson was closing in on the first of her two Boston Marathon wins when she asked a spectator how far it was to Heartbreak Hill. "Lady," the spectator replied, "you just passed it."

But for every Samuelson, there were a hundred marathoners whose dreams died on Heartbreak. The hill rose at the very point where a runner's glycogen stores neared bottom and exhaustion was approaching. The long, steady decline in elevation during the first half of the course had already strained the quadriceps, and now came a series of sharp ascents and descents. If the previous three hills served in the metaphorical role of picadors, softening a marathoner up for the kill, then Heartbreak Hill represented the matador with his fatal sword.

The huge crowds jamming Commonwealth Avenue that day made the hill especially difficult to distinguish. "The crowds were unbelievable," Beardsley remembered in his autobiography. "There was no crowd control. After our race, they finally got some, but that day there was none. As we went through the hills, there was maybe enough room for Salazar and me to run side by side if we would have wanted to, but that was about it. People on each side of the street could have reached out and touched people on the other side. . . . It was so thick with spectators you couldn't even see how the hills went up. It was just this mass of humanity, people hanging out of trees or whatever."

Beardsley remained reasonably confident; if Salazar had a commanding, preemptive card to play, he would have shown it by now. Dick sensed that Alberto was firing on all cylinders just to stay up with him (of course, the same could be said of Dick). Despite the heat, moreover, Salazar had consumed very little water over the course of the race. Beardsley continued to drink freely from the cups and bottles offered by spectators. He would drink, pour water over his painter's cap, and wet down a sponge he kept in his waistband to douse his head as he ran. He knew a lot of tricks. Although Salazar had run two of the greatest marathons in history, those were his only two marathons. Beardsley had run 15.

"In many ways, I was the exact opposite of Salazar," he said. "I hardly ever set foot on the track, not even for speedwork. I did all my fast training during long road runs. The 20-mile run was my specialty. I would do fartleks and intervals, practice surging and tempo stuff, all during 20-mile road workouts. If you look at my track times, such as they were, you'd never think I could run marathons as fast as I did. You're supposed to run a sub-28-minute 10-K in order to run a sub-2:10 marathon. Well, the fall before Boston, I ran a 10-K PR of 29:02, and I was ecstatic. But something happened to me when I got in a marathon. Especially those miles from 17 to 21. That's the point in a marathon when most guys are really hurting, when they're most vulnerable. But that's when I felt my strongest. I would kick in from 17 to 21 and make guys really, really hurt."

Just as Salazar went against the common wisdom of the sport by training so intensely, Beardsley challenged it by his constant racing. Most elite distance runners ran no more than two marathons per year; 6 months was considered the minimum recovery and preparation period to run a first-rate marathon. For the last 3 years, however, Beardsley had been averaging a marathon every 8 to 10 weeks. He rarely turned down an invitation to race. He needed the money, he enjoyed the travel and competition, and he didn't have to worry about peaking for an Olympics or world championships. He also had a great deal of trouble saying no.

Indeed, in many ways, Beardsley was exactly the athlete that Salazar thought—an honorable journeyman. Yet he was also more than that.

"Dickie had the most beautiful, efficient style I ever saw," Squires said. "When you watched Dickie run, violins played and little birdies flew around. He had this fluid forefoot-striking stride that was almost effortless. Alberto was a mess by comparison. But it didn't matter because Alberto was such a tiger, he could stand so much pain. But Dickie was a monster in his own right. When he first came to me, I thought, 'Christ, this guy must've been a beast in college; how come I never heard of him?' But when he showed me his college times, I couldn't believe how bad they were. Shit, who'd been coaching this kid, Parson Brown? The guy was so strong—I mean literally strong. He was a farmer, for chrissakes. Dickie was a tough, tough guy."

Besides strength, Beardsley also brought an impressive depth of feeling to his sport. "I've never been the slightest bit bored with running," he wrote in his autobiography. "I don't consider hard work and great fun mutually exclusive. Who decided that anyway? A lot of people say they love running because of how they feel afterward. Not me. Well, I love that, too, but it's also so much fun while I'm out there. I used to be able to run 30 miles averaging a 5:30, 5:40 pace the entire time and never be tempted to quit. You start pounding out a couple dozen 5- or 6-minute miles and you start to feel such a sense of satisfaction and peace you can't believe it. Sure you're tired, and sure you're sore, but if you could bottle the high you get from transcending the pain mile after mile after mile, well . . . reality was overrated."

As the hills unreeled, Beardsley launched one gambit after another. He would drive hard for 400 yards, then back off for 200. He'd repeat the cycle two or three times. But after a third fast 400, he'd slow down for only 100 yards. Then, hoping to catch Salazar flat-footed, he would surge.

But Salazar covered every move. He stayed plastered on Beardsley's shoulder. "Although I didn't really feel tired or sore, I didn't feel smooth," Salazar told reporters afterward. "I wasn't concerned with what Beardsley was trying to do. I was just concentrating on staying with him. I kept telling myself, 'There's no way I'm going to lose this race.' Those last 7 miles, my only thought was to keep up with him. If I could do that, I knew I'd win. My attitude changed during the race from going for a really good time to just having a clear victory to finally just winning."

Beardsley, meanwhile, kept watching Salazar's shadow on the asphalt. "The shadow never disappeared," he would recall. "I couldn't get rid of it. It's kind of awesome to have a shadow trailing you."

Heartbreak Hill came and went. The two runners remained joined.

Alberto Salazar was 2 years old when his family left Cuba in 1960. His direct memories of the island were spectral and disjointed. Sunshine splashing through a window, a breeze moving a curtain, a snatch of music off the street, the palm trees receding as the plane lifted off for the brief but epochal flight to Miami. Still, Cuba dominated Alberto's childhood and youth, coloring his life more vividly than if his family had stayed on the devil's island.

At school in America, they called him Castro Convertible. He didn't like it, didn't understand it. He just wanted to be like the other kids. On the streets and at school, it was all American English, but at home, it was Spanish completely. Later in high school when he'd started winning races, he told the reporter his name was Albert Salazar, which is how it appeared in the local paper. That sent his father into a rage. From that day forward, he was strictly, unalterably Alberto.

The boy heard the old-country stories so often that it seemed like they had happened to him. It was almost as if Alberto, and not his father, had saved Fidel Castro's life that day in Havana in 1951. The two young men had been undergraduates at the University of Havana. Jose Salazar studied engineering, Castro the law. They both came from upper-class Spanish families.

Fidel was born out of wedlock to a wealthy planter from Oriente Province; Jose descended from an aristocratic line of doctors, lawyers, engineers, and soldiers in Havana. A brilliant speaker and charismatic leader, Castro picked up the flag of the revered rebel patriot Jose Martí.

"Let those who desire a secure homeland conquer it," Martí wrote. "Let those who do not conquer it live under the whip and in exile, watched over like wild animals, cast from one country to another, concealing the death of their souls with a beggar's smile from the scorn of free men."

Castro recognized that Cuba had become the harlot of the Yankees and that Fulgencio Batista, the Cuban president, was no better than the Americans' pimp. Fidel vowed to restore Cuba's honor, scour away the corruption. Every young Cuban man with spirit, intelligence, and nerve joined Fidel's cause.

In the prerevolution 1950s, the University of Havana was a snake pit of political ferment and intrigue. Impassioned young men stoked on strong, black, sugary coffee formed alliances—in effect, gangs—who slashed and shot and visited general mayhem on their rivals. Politically motivated murders occurred regularly on campus. Only young men of unwavering courage and resolve rose to positions of leadership. Jose was elected to represent the engineering school in the student congress; Fidel, the law school. They were friends according to the old Cuban code, which could often mean friends to the death.

So on that day in 1951 when the government agents or members of a rival gang or Batista's soldiers (Alberto was never sure which group exactly; it was all so complicated and had happened so long ago, and his father grew so agitated when he tried to explain the details) arrived on campus to arrest or kill Fidel, Jose gave his friend refuge in his office. Outside the building, a campus policeman confronted the attackers. *Fidel is no friend of mine, but Jose Salazar is my friend and therefore you shall not pass.*

A stalemate ensued. The day passed with Jose and Fidel hiding in the darkened office, peeking out through the blinds, waiting to hear their attackers' boots drumming in the hallway. But the boots never sounded, and when night came, Fidel escaped from Jose's office and into history. The story had been repeated and burnished so many times over the years that Alberto almost felt like Fidel Castro was an uncle or grandfather or some other relative out of the family's distant but resonant Cuban past.

Alberto's father had helped save Castro's life. He had fought beside Fidel and Che Guevara in the Sierra Maestra. He rode a tank as the *Fidelistas* rolled triumphantly into Havana just after New Years 1959. For the next 18 months, Jose Salazar had faithfully served the revolutionary government, contributing his civil engineering skills to a total of 49 projects, including hotels, housing developments, and national parks. But during that time, Jose watched with growing dismay as Castro, isolated and threatened by the Americans and seduced by the promise of Soviet support, seemed to turn away from the democratic ideals of the revolution. Castro canceled elections and swept aside any man who stood in his way. While delivering succor to the country's long-oppressed peasants, he ignored the teachers, physicians, managers, and engineers who made Cuba work, and families of impeccable bourgeois pedigree, such as the Salazars. Jose watched Castro take more and more from his family and friends.

"One of my father's major efforts was a community development project—a model village to be constructed in one of the provinces," Alberto wrote in a 1983 article published in the magazine *Guideposts.* "By 1960 it was finished except for one building—the chapel. But then my father was told not to go ahead with that church. In fact, a government order forbade him to start construction. And that's when, he's told me, he realized that his friend Castro was becoming more and more a Communist, and turning Cuba into a Marxist state, a state without God."

It was a state in which Jose Salazar, like many other former Castro comrades, decided he could no longer reside. "I left Cuba on October 12, 1960," he says. "My aides warned me not to tell Fidel because he would kill me. But I wasn't worried."

Jose left behind a family home and inheritance. He landed in Miami with nothing but a few hundred dollars. A few weeks later, his wife and four children joined him. In Florida, Jose immersed himself in the campaign to overthrow Castro. For 6 weeks, he trained in the Everglades for the Bay of Pigs invasion, planning to land with the second wave (the CIA organizers were suspicious of former *Fidelistas,* suspecting some might be double agents, and thus held them in reserve). But the second wave never embarked for Cuba. Castro's forces smashed the invasion. The debacle seared the hearts of the exiles, who felt betrayed by President Kennedy and the CIA.

Jose Salazar turned to making a new life in America. He found work with a civil engineering firm in Connecticut that later transferred him to Massachusetts. The family moved into the house in Wayland, not far from the midway point of the Boston Marathon course. But while his destiny turned increasingly American, Jose's heart stayed with Cuba. He dedicated every spare moment to overthrowing the Castro regime, joining the campaign for a second invasion that was tantalizingly promised by a succession of US administrations but never enacted. "Next Year in Havana" was the vow Alberto's father lived by.

Jose rose to a position of leadership in New England's Cuban exile community, presiding over frequent meetings at the family house. "In the continuing opera still called, even by Cubans who have now lived the largest part of their lives in this country, *el exilio,* the exile, meetings at private houses are seen to have consequences," Joan Didion explained in the book *Miami,* published in 1987. "The actions of individuals are seen to affect events directly."

Alberto grew up with angry men shouting in Spanish around the dining room table. Cigar and cigarette smoke thickened the air. One time, he remembers, a man stalked out of the house and came back in carrying a machine gun. Besides the seven members of the immediate Salazar family (Alberto's youngest brother, Fernando, was born in 1965), the household included seven exiled Cuban cousins. Born to a grand Havana style, the extended family now scraped to get by. The change wasn't so wrenching for Jose because of his furious energy and indomitable will. But it fell to Marta Salazar, Alberto's mother, raised in old-world gentility, to cook and scrub and wash and mend for more than a dozen people in a modest house. She suffered through the interminable New England winters. Marta also longed for Havana, but in a more mournful key than her husband.

One day, the news arrived from Cuba that Jose's mother had died. Jose feared that Castro's men would arrest him—or perhaps try to kill him—upon his return to the island. So Jose acquired a handgun for protection on his journey. That is the story of how the gun came into the house.

Jose kept the gun in a cupboard above the refrigerator. Five-year-old Alberto was drawn to the firearm as if to a cookie jar. One day, when his mother was busy elsewhere in the house, he climbed up on the kitchen counter, reached above the refrigerator, and removed the gun from the cupboard. Alberto was gazing down its blue barrel when Ricardo happened into the kitchen and took the gun away from his little brother. Neither boy breathed a word about the episode. Later, when their father came home, he took the gun down to the basement, where he had jury-rigged a firing range using an old mattress. Jose squeezed the trigger and a round discharged. Only by grace had Alberto been spared.

His father was devoted and loving but also querulous, dogmatic, and demanding. He was obsessed with Fidel Castro on the one hand and making his mark in America on the other. He expected his daughter and four sons to live up to the highest standards of both Cuban and American conduct. The Salazar children were required to both blend in and stand out. When Alberto tried to skip an awards ceremony because he finished only third in a race, his father drove him back to the stadium. He made Alberto accept the award and say thank you, sir. By the same token, when Alberto told his father that an opposing runner had intentionally tripped him during a race, Jose had returned to the track to confront the runner and his father.

"I recall an air of tension around the house," says Kirk Pfrangle. "It wasn't always a comfortable place to be. Alberto's father often seemed angry and preoccupied with Castro. Al and his father used to get into terrible arguments. I always wanted to get in and out of there as quickly as possible."

Cajoled by his father, inspired by his older brother, and driven by his own hunger to excel, Alberto developed into a top student and one of the most promising American distance-running prospects since the Jim Ryun era of the 1960s. While still in high school, Salazar set a national junior record for the 2-mile run and logged a pair of victories in the 5000 meters at US-USSR junior track meets. Bill Dellinger deliberately refrained from visiting the homes of University of Oregon distance-running recruits, allowing his program's legendary reputation to speak for him. But he made an exception in Alberto's case. When Dellinger arrived with his scholarship offer, it promised deliverance on several planes: It was a way for Alberto to develop his running to the highest level, a way to please and honor his father, and a way perhaps to put an entire continent between his father and himself.

Alberto stayed in Oregon through the years of his athletic ascendancy and remained there through the mysterious, dispiriting years of his decline. Just as his father lived a double life, prospering in a professional career while at the same time clinging to his role as exile and devoting himself to the quixotic task of returning to Cuba, Alberto had his twin projects. The world regarded him as a successful businessman and happy family man. In his own eyes, however, he was frustrated and depressed. Clinging to his role as a great distance runner, he devoted himself to the quixotic task of resuming his athletic career. Like his father, whose heart lay in the homeland he would likely never regain, Alberto defined himself not by what he possessed but by what he had lost.

The years passed, and Salazar's running triumphs, which once seemed simultaneously indelible and suggestive of even greater triumphs to come, grew distant and abstract. He had two sons of his own now. In fact, one of the few activities that Alberto wholeheartedly enjoyed, in which he could temporarily lose himself, was coaching his son Alejandro's youth soccer team. In general, however, Salazar was distracted, surly, and gloomy.

"I worried about Alberto during those years," says Kirk Pfrangle. "He was so different than The Rookie, the kid I'd known back in Boston. Most of the time, he seemed moody and angry. Other times, it seemed like he wasn't even there. Those were the times that really concerned me. Finally, we just sort of stopped talking. Alberto drifted away, and I wondered if we would ever get him back."

Salazar refused to acknowledge his depression to Molly, to his friends, or even to himself. He did not seek help. He didn't go to a therapist. Such conduct, he thought, would be unbecoming of a man. A man—especially a machismo-steeped Cuban man—dealt with his own problems. He remained stoic in the face of adversity. He did his job, accepted his fate, did not whine or complain. A man stood on his own two feet and took care of his family. That was the code that Alberto had learned from his own father. He didn't need anybody to help guide him out of his darkness—including his father. He certainly didn't need any of his father's Virgin Mary moonshine.

Alberto had been getting the packets regularly through the late 1980s, manila envelopes thick with tracts, articles, and testimonials concerning Medjugorje, a remote village in the Balkans of Yugoslavia. There, on a June afternoon in 1981, six local teenagers reported that they had encountered an apparition of the Virgin Mary. The youths claimed that they had walked up a hill after serving communion for the local Franciscan priests and had witnessed a woman of shining aspect who identified herself as Gospa, or the Holy Mother. The figure had spoken to the youths for a few minutes, then departed. The teenagers immediately reported the occurrence to the parish priests. In subsequent days, they reported that the figure returned to them individually each afternoon. The six young people fell into trances, during which the apparition instructed them. Upon wakening, they announced the teachings, which consisted of gentle, motherly reminders to pray, say the rosary, attend Mass and confession, observe the sacraments, fast 2 days a week, and obey the Pope.

The news of the reported apparitions raised a sensation. Word burned through the Croat-dominated Herzegovina region of Yugoslavia, where the Franciscan order of the Roman Catholic Church had served the villages since the 15th century, when the area was under Turkish rule. The church now coexisted, not always smoothly, with the present Communist government. Croats from surrounding villages and the nearby city of Mostar flocked to Medjugorje to hear the children's witness and experience what they claimed to be their own holy encounters. When government officials tried to suppress the movement, it only grew more popular, spreading to Western Europe. Thousands of pilgrims were soon arriving from Italy, France, Spain, and the United States. Medjugorje prayer groups, aligned with the charismatic movement in the Roman Catholic Church, formed in nations around the world. Early in 1985, a Medjugorje witness spoke at the St. Zepherin's Catholic Church in Wayland, Massachusetts, where Jose Salazar was a member and communicant.

The testimony struck an immediate chord with Jose, who was already well disposed toward saints, miracles, and other aspects of the charismatic movement. He was a devout Catholic of the Cuban-Exile variety, in which orthodox faith intertwined with rabid anti-Communism. In fact, the Cuban exiles had built their own chapel on the beach in Miami and whose front door looked to Havana, 90 miles distant. The joke was that the chapel was situated so the exiles' prayers carried straight across the Caribbean and up the trousers of Fidel's fatigues. That the Holy Mother would call to her children from Yugoslavia, a largely peasant nation governed by Communists and seething with barely suppressed medieval hatreds, did not seem at all fantastic to Jose Salazar. Indeed, the story spoke directly to his exile's heart.

In 1987, Jose embarked on his own pilgrimage to Medjugorje. He came home breathing Gospa-inspired fire, raving how the chain holding his rosary beads had miraculously turned from silver to gold and how the Holy Spirit seemed to seep from the village's very soil. Even Marta Salazar, a sober, no-nonsense woman, vouched for the rosary-bead phenomenon. Now, almost weekly, another fat envelope arrived from Massachusetts, jammed with clippings, tracts, and articles and a scribbled plea from Jose to study and pray over the material.

"Alberto had always been the most devout of my four children," Jose Salazar explains, "but also the one most in need of grace."

Alberto threw the stuff into a corner of his office and didn't give it a thought. He was a serious man of affairs, meeting the payroll of a big, splashy, prime-rib-and-seafood joint with a dark cocktail lounge where, during happy hour, both town and gown big shots cut deals over their microbrews. He had to keep after the hippie kids working for him to make sure they weren't snorting coke or worse in the restrooms. Moreover, he still held the title of Greatest American Distance Runner. Nobody had come along to challenge him, and Alberto was determined to defend his throne. If he kept searching, kept seeking out doctors, coaches, chiropractors, massage therapists, and nutritionists, Salazar still might hit on a cure. Against steadily rising odds, the formerly great distance runner desperately sought a silver bullet, which he would ride to a glory so radiant that even Fidel Castro would hear of his exploits and stroke his graying beard in wonder.

Alberto had always been a good Catholic. He attended Mass, gave talks to church youth groups, and baptized his sons. He didn't go overboard like his old man, praying a hole through each day; but compared to most people his age—especially out in pagan, Deadhead Eugene—he was practically an altar boy. As with most other central themes in his life, Alberto's faith derived from his father.

As a kid in Wayland, it seemed like Alberto spent all his time in church. His parents were passionately faithful. When you went to mass with Jose, you knew he was concentrating; and when Marta observed the sacraments, it was with her whole heart.

When he went away to Oregon, Alberto poured his spiritual energy into his sport. He remained an observant Catholic but kept a more or less typical college-boy distance from the church, until the Falmouth Road Race in 1978. Although the course was only 7.1 miles long (and was laid out by race organizer Tommy Leonard to pass the shore town's most popular taverns), Falmouth was run in mid-August, at the height of the summer's heat and humidity. It was the main event of New England's summer running season. The entire Boston running community, including Bill Squires and all of the Greater Boston Track Club, traveled to Cape Cod for the weekend. Bill Rodgers had been 30 at the time, still in his prime, while Alberto had been just 20 and about to begin his junior year at the University of Oregon.

Salazar wanted to prove his mettle to his old teammates, show them that he was no longer The Rookie. Rodgers, for his part, wanted to put the upstart kid in his place. Rodgers steamed to the lead, and Salazar went with him for about 6 miles. In the boiling heat, however, Alberto eventually withered to a 10th-place finish. Just past the finish line, he turned white and collapsed from dehydration and heat exhaustion.

He was rushed into the medical tent. They packed ice around him, but his temperature kept rocketing. Alberto was semidelirious. Was he hallucinating, or were these voices real? One hundred four and rising. . .a hundred five. . .a hundred six. . .

He must have drifted off, because a priest stood over him pronouncing the last rites of the church. That had to be a dream. He blinked his eyes, but the priest was still there. The doctors moved frantically now.

Alberto closed his eyes.

When he opened them, the priest was gone, and his father stood in his place. "Alberto," he said, "Alberto, look at this." He held two small pieces of wood together in the shape of a cross. They might have been tongue depressors or some other ordinary pieces of wood that were lying around. His father had made them into a cross. In a strong steady voice, his father said, "Look at the cross, Alberto. Pray with me. Hail Mary full of grace. . ."

"Constancy is a quality that the dictionary defines as 'a steadiness of mind under duress,'" Alberto wrote, concluding the *Guideposts* article. "My father had shown that quality when he opposed Castro [he was true to his faith]; he had shown it to me dramatically when he put together that makeshift cross and caused me to summon again my faith."

Now, years later, that story seemed to have been written by another person—a much younger, happier, less cynical, and more hopeful man. His father, meanwhile, had grown increasingly hidebound in his orthodoxy, ranting about the Holy Mother skydiving into some little village in Yugoslavia. This was bizarre, even by Jose's standards.

Or was it? As with other Marian apparition sites such as Lourdes in France and Fatima in Portugal, Medjugorje had become a seat for reported miracles and divine intercession. If Alberto was ever going to run well again, a miracle—one even more dramatic than what had occurred in the medical tent in Falmouth—was practically required. He had not yet tried miracle therapy.

So one day, Alberto turned to the pile of envelopes gathering dust in the corner of his office. Leafing through their contents, he was struck by the directness, simplicity, and touching awkwardness of the material. There was nothing smooth or slick here, no vague amorphous junk about social justice and self-realization or other mainstream church boilerplate. Instead, there were a lot of capital letters and exclamation marks.

This was all first-hand testimony, and it came from kids. The crux of the matter was the veracity of the six teenagers who were visited daily by the Gospa (on a complex revolving schedule that must have required a divine appointments secretary to keep straight). The language was clumsily translated from the Slavic tongue, but it was clear and specific. Nothing hifalutin, just go back to the basics. Here's what you do: Pray this way each day, fast this way 2 days a week, go to Mass and confession. Satan exists. He is real because the Holy Mother is real and incarnate, appearing mild and loving and knowing to the children. And this was her voice.

Alberto read with absorption and a building sense of excitement. He felt an itching in his limbs, as if he wanted to run. But at the same time, he couldn't move. Time passed, but Alberto wasn't aware of it. These teachings seemed precisely tuned to his longings.

I am real, children. Come to the mother. Do not appeal to the unyielding, unapproachable father. I understand, children. Come to me. Your mother loves you and will shelter you and show you the way. And the way was the fundamentals. Pray without ceasing. Seems hard seems unattainable well no harder than 140 miles per week no harder than the Boston Marathon against Dick Beardsley 9 days after running 27:30 against Henry Rono. There were steps you could take. Satan was real. Of course he was— Alberto had grown up with him. The devil Fidel Castro had lived in his house in Wayland, Massachusetts, less than a mile away from the Boston Marathon course. Now, in a mountain village on the far side of the world, the Holy Mother had appeared to beat the devil. Here are the stones to throw against him, children.

Alberto studied the faces of the Medjugorje children. They were not like American faces—soft, greedy faces expecting something for nothing. These children were not like the naive American kids who still thought that Fidel and Che were romantic revolutionary heroes. Alberto's father had known Che and told this story: One day in the Sierra Maestra, Che had happened across a group of badly wounded government soldiers left to suffer in the sun with no water. A comrade had lifted his rifle to put them out of their misery. An act of mercy. But Che ordered the comrade to put up his rifle, saying, don't waste the bullet; these men are not worth the lead. He left the soldiers to suffer agonizing deaths. That was the romantic Che whose poster looked down from all those dormitory walls at the University of Oregon.

These Medjugorje kids were not like the Americans. For all their trusting, they were not naive. Their testimony made Alberto's heart quicken. There was something here, something undoubtedly.

A few months later, Alberto, Molly, and their two boys boarded a flight to Yugoslavia.

Beardsley came off Heartbreak Hill with Salazar breathing down his neck. The crowds pressed so close that there was barely a path to run through. They were screaming so loud that he couldn't hear himself think. He couldn't feel his legs. They seemed to belong to somebody else.

In the course of all his marathons and in all the thousands of miles he'd covered in other races and workouts around the world—from a gravel road along the St. Croix River on the Minnesota-Wisconsin border to the London Bridge across the Thames—Dick thought he'd seen, heard, touched, and felt everything possible. He'd been chased by dogs. The skin between his thighs had chafed until he bled. His muscles had cramped into iron. Opponents had knocked him down, and he had knocked down opponents. He'd been snowed on, rained on, hailed on, scorched and frozen, and raked by tempest winds. He had taken wrong turns. He had run superbly, wretchedly, and indifferently, but he had never, ever felt phantomlike pillars of air where his legs ought to be.

This couldn't be good. But it couldn't be all that bad, because he was still moving, still leading. In fact, Beardsley and Salazar were cooking through the Newton Hills faster than any runners had ever done before at the Boston Marathon. They made the 4-mile journey in 19 minutes and 11 seconds, more than a minute faster than the 20:45 checkpoint record set by Bill Rodgers en route to his 1978 victory. The stately paced first half of the race, during which Rodgers could joke about canoes and pretty girls, was long gone. A dream from a past life. Or was this the dream?

The crowd's noise sucked his breath away yet at the same time filled him up. They weren't just cheering for Alberto anymore; they were cheering for Beardsley, too. The people knew that they were watching something special. Two guys who couldn't lose each other, who maybe never would lose each other. It was as if Alberto and he had started the hills as separate men and come out of them the same man. Before the hills, he could feel his legs, but now his legs were gone.

Twenty-one miles into the 86th Boston Marathon, and he was running a stride in front of the great Salazar. Five more miles. That was unthinkable. Beardsley decided he'd just go 1 more mile. That would be easy—or at least possible. Stay ahead of the shadow for 1 more mile. After that—well, he'd think of something.

He couldn't feel his legs. One more mile.

Alberto Salazar, by contrast, felt every quivering muscle fiber in his legs. Shards of pain splintered up from Alberto's left hamstring. The pain was growing very difficult to suppress. It was Salazar's conviction that a runner should honor and respect pain, come to know it in all of its aspects, but ultimately deny it.

The most famous example of his ability to deny pain, of course, had come at the Falmouth race in 1978, when he'd been so overheated and dehydrated that he was administered the last rites of the Catholic Church, and his father, standing above him with the makeshift cross, had delivered the seeming miracle.

From that race, his legend was born. Alberto Salazar would run to the point of death. "A lot of people asked me, 'Well, are you going to be scared to push yourself again?' I wasn't," he told a reporter later. "That fall, I broke through tremendously. It was completely from that Falmouth race. I won the NCAA cross-country championship and continued to improve. So Falmouth was a turning point in my career. It just made me mentally tougher."

Drawing on his experience in Falmouth, Salazar now confronted the heat and pain of Boston. He found that with the pulsing of his hamstring, the heat no longer bothered him. He felt no need for water. In fact, sometime during the last few miles, he had stopped sweating. His singlet had stiffened as if covered in dried blood.

"It was a whole different game once we got to the hills," Salazar would tell reporters. "We had been running really slow, and from my point of view that was fine. But once we started up, he began pushing the pace at an intensity that neither of us could continue to the finish. It was a matter of time before either he would break me, or he would have to slow down himself."

The crowds didn't matter. His time didn't matter, nor did his eventual margin of victory. Beardsley didn't matter. All that mattered now was not losing. Salazar could forget about everything else and focus on that single and sovereign goal. He might lose a 10,000-meter match race to a Henry Rono, but he did not lose marathons, especially to a palooka in a painter's cap. Any moment now, Beardsley might blow up and drop away like a disintegrating booster rocket. If he could maintain the pace until the end, then it would simply be a matter of outkicking him.

Alberto Salazar feared no opponent, at least none that he could see.

13

Dick Beardsley's 50-yard walk across the Kmart parking lot seemed longer and more difficult than his crawl across the barnyard of Bloom Lake Farm after the PTO accident. It certainly seemed harder than any marathon. When he finally made it inside the store's automatic doors, Beardsley paused for a moment to gather himself, let the air-conditioning dry the nervous sweat misting his forehead. Kmart's familiar floor-wax and fresh-plastic aromas, along with its gaudy welter of merchandise and the riverlike din of shoppers, reassured him, but only for a moment. As the doors hissed close behind him, his paranoia returned. He presumed he was under surveillance. Special high-tech cameras, primed to detect waves of fear and anxiety, were no doubt zeroing in on him. He imagined store detectives observing him from behind one-way windows. He knew what he ought to do: turn around and flee the store. Instead, he turned to his left and, as casually as possible, walked 30 feet down the store's central aisle to the pharmacy.

Kmart put the pharmacy near the door for the convenience of its senior-citizen customers. There were a lot of older people living in the Fargo/Moorhead area, gnarled Scandinavian farmers and retirees from the Twin Cities, although the latter mostly headed south by autumn's first hard frost. Many of these old-timers filled their prescriptions here, and Dick liked to shoot the breeze with them while waiting for his pills. The pharmacists often shared jokes while handing Dick his medicine. He always enjoyed his trips to Kmart. But on every previous visit to the store's pharmacy, no matter how deviously he had wheedled them, his prescriptions had been legal.

He approached the reception desk and, with all the aplomb he could muster, handed the forged prescription for Demerol to the clerk. She did not return his smile. She took the slip straight back to the druggist. This was different, wasn't it? Didn't the clerk usually put the slips in an in-box?

The druggist was a man Dick often dealt with. He glanced at the prescription, then looked at Dick, who grinned and waved, thinking that it was all over. The cops were going to be on top of him in a heartbeat.

"Okay," the clerk said to him. "It'll just be 10 or 15 minutes."

With a rocketing heart, Beardsley wandered the aisles, staring at dust mops, camcorders, coffeemakers, and basketballs but seeing nothing. He did not belong here. He belonged at home with Mary and Andy, packing to go see his father for the last time. Instead, he roamed the aisles of Kmart, looking toward the pharmacy counter every 5 seconds, praying for the bag with his pills to appear, expecting the hard hand of the law on his shoulder.

The hand, however, never fell. Dick looked up and there, on the counter, sat a white bag with his name on it. A little sack of bliss. He went to claim his trophy—Lord knows, he'd worked hard enough for it—still half-expecting it to be snatched away at the last moment. But the clerk merely rang up the sale. Dick's druggist buddy grinned, waved, and told him to have a good one.

Beardsley now possessed 60 precious hits of Demerol. As he climbed back into his truck, he felt a surge of well-being that was almost as good as the drug itself. The worry and guilt drained out of him like dirty water out of a bathtub. Anything this easy couldn't really be illegal, he told himself. He needn't feel afraid or ashamed.

He drove across the mall parking lot to the Wal-Mart and, on his first attempt, scribbled another dead-on forgery. He sailed into the store, projecting strong, confident vibes, and sailed out 10 minutes later with 60 more pills. Dick was on a roll. Next stop was Target, whose pharmacy was unfamiliar to him. The druggist there studied the prescription, then eyed Beardsley. "Okay," he said. "But since you're a new customer, you have to fill out this form."

Dick completed the form with a steady hand, displaying a calm demeanor; so that the druggist would no more suspect him than he would Mister Rogers. He handed in the form, and a few minutes later, a third white bag magically materialized. Another 60 shots of happiness.

On the drive home, Beardsley stopped at a small drugstore in Detroit Lakes and forged still another prescription. He filled it without difficulty and came out of the store whistling. The next morning, he set off for Michigan with 240 hits of Demerol riding in his truck's glove compartment. Stoned as a rock star, with Dolly Parton on the tape deck and a Diet Coke in the beverage holder, Dick steered into the rising sun, equably negotiating with the higher powers.

"Just get me through Dad's funeral, Lord, and then I promise I'll quit."

When he started home 8 days later after his father's funeral, there were three pills remaining. On his way out of town he stopped at his dad's house, hotfooted for the bathroom medicine cabinet, rifling it for painkillers. Dad had gotten a lot for the cancer, but dammit the pills were gone. His sister Maryann had gotten there ahead of him and flushed them all. He popped the last of his Moorhead pills and drove balls-to-the-wall back home. He would process all this later deal with Dad's death later now he just had to drive hard fast across Michigan across Wisconsin hitting Minnesota at Duluth near midnight. He found an all-night drugstore took a few deep breaths to steady himself forged his prescription did the job inside and came back to the truck recalling the bargain he'd struck so cavalierly at the start of his journey. He gulped down the pills thinking, Lord, I'm sorry, but the deal is off.

Dick got home and just sort of went crazy. By the end of the summer, he was taking 90 tablets a day. To avoid suspicion, he would fill the forged prescriptions on a circuit of a dozen pharmacies within a 20-mile radius of Detroit Lakes. This required a great deal of work and planning, but that fact didn't bother Beardsley. If he'd worked and planned as a distance runner, dairy farmer, and fishing guide, he could work and plan as a dope addict. He didn't do things part-time or halfway. He was going to be the best darn dope addict around.

Beardsley spent all his waking moments thinking about pills—acquiring them, concealing them—much in the way that, years earlier, in the month before the 1982 Boston Marathon, he spent all his time thinking about Alberto Salazar. Demerol was his preferred high, but he mixed in prescriptions for Percocet and Valium to lend an air of authenticity to his forgeries. With meticulous care, he recorded his drug transactions in a small notebook, disguising the entries as bait purchases for his fishing guide business. He also cultivated other means of supply. When Mary and Dick visited a friend's house for dinner, Dick excused himself from the table, went to the bathroom, and rummaged through his host's medicine cabinet for pain pills. On one occasion, he even copped pills from Carole Ross, the mother of his best friend in Wayzata, the woman who helped raise him.

"One day, during the worst of his troubles, Dick showed up at my house," Ross recalled. "He told me he had a terrible toothache and that he'd driven over from Detroit Lakes to see his dentist in St. Paul. He looked tired and nervous. There was no doubt he was suffering.

"He said to me, 'Carole, do you have anything around here that might take the edge off until I make it to my appointment?'

"I sort of knew what he was after. My husband, Joe, had recently died from colon cancer. Joe's cancer had been very painful, and doctors had given him a lot of powerful drugs. Dick was hoping that there would still be some of Joe's pills around the house. The first thing I did after he died was flush them all. But I had some pills of my own that a doctor had prescribed for arthritis. Dick just looked so miserable. I did something I shouldn't have—I gave him three or four of my pain pills."

By the end of the summer of 1996, Beardsley was sounding the bottom. "I would finish a day's work, come home and eat dinner, go to bed, and get up at one o'clock in the morning to take pills and stare at the TV," he said. "Although by this time, there was no more pleasure in it. I wasn't taking the pills to get high but to avoid withdrawal. I couldn't sleep. I'd get these splitting headaches. My ears would ring. I would take some pills, which would give me a 20-minute break. Then the headaches would start again, I'd pop more pills, and so on. My stomach burned. I chugged Maalox straight from the bottle like it was Gatorade."

In September, the Dick Beardsley Half-Marathon came around again. Somehow, he was able to function throughout the race weekend. Each day, he took more and more pills. "I was just totally out of control," he said. "Every 3 or 4 days, I would fill a prescription for 50 to 100 pills. I took money from my business to pay for them. It never crossed my mind that the prescriptions weren't legitimate. In my sick little mind, they were as real as they could be."

Amazingly, Beardsley was able to hide his disease, live a double life. He appeared to be the same great guy as always—friendly, generous, outgoing, forthright, not the least bit pompous despite his past as a world-class athlete. His fishing guide business was thriving, as was his public-speaking sideline.

That summer, he was invited to speak at a dairy industry conference. A half hour before his talk, he downed a few Percocet. Then he stood up before an audience of a thousand and gave the best talk of his life. His stories had the people rolling in the aisles. When he described the '82 Boston against Salazar, they were on the edges of their seats. But in the middle of his presentation, he came to a dead halt. He couldn't think of what to say next. So he told the first story that popped into his head. A thousand faces stared up at him. He went cold. My God, he thought, had he already told them this one?

At the bait shop or on a boat with a client, Beardsley never slurred his words or stumbled. He drove with obsessive care. He hid his pills in a secret place in his pickup truck and floated around in a private, secret cloud that insulated him from all trouble and anxiety. He was a week or two away from dying.

"After I got caught, during detox and treatment, the doctors just shook their heads when they found out how much I was taking," Beardsley said. "It was enough to kill an elephant. The doctors said that thanks to my running, I had a tremendously rapid metabolism and an incredibly strong heart. Still, it was only a matter of time until one morning I just wouldn't wake up."

At home in the evenings, Dick would often nod off over his

supper plate. One night, Mary said to him in frustration, "Do you think you could force yourself to stay awake and watch a video with me tonight?"

Worried that his cover might be fraying, he willed himself to watch the entire movie. The next day, while returning the video to the rental shop, he decided to surprise Mary with another movie. He spent a long time combing the aisles, studying various titles. Finally, he found a film he was sure she would like.

At home, when he delivered the surprise, Mary stared at him. The video he had brought her was the same one they had watched the night before.

14

Dick Beardsley still couldn't feel his legs. But mile 24 had passed, so his 1-more-mile scheme seemed to be working.

He kept watching Salazar's shadow. For a solid hour, he'd been watching the head bobbing and arm flying, sensing his opponent without looking at him, yet seeing him even more clearly from this refracted angle. He knew that Salazar was hurting, digging way down deep, as deep as Beardsley was. Maybe Alberto had lost touch with some part of himself, too. The two men were running together into new territory.

It was like the first time Dick had taken his skiff across Lake Minnetonka. He had been 11 or 12 at the time. At some points, the lake was 3 miles wide. Forty years earlier, stern-wheeled ferry boats worked Minnetonka, steaming to Excelsior Amusement Park or to the grand hotels where wealthy tourists from the East spent whole summers. There were casinos in the hotels where the rich people gambled. Babe Ruth once visited Lake Minnetonka.

It was a big lake, and crossing it for the first time gave the boy pause. Dick steered the skiff deep into the heart of the water. He was afraid to look back because he knew the familiar shore would be out of sight. He was afraid to lift his eyes and look toward the horizon because . . . well, there were a hundred reasons to fear the shore ahead.

The push the not-feeling the pounding the din from the crowd like an ocean roaring and the shadow always in front of him. Sometimes it seemed like the shadow was leading and pulling him along rather than vice versa. He just had to stay with the shadow.

Suddenly the shadow swelled grotesquely, looming behind him like a monster. He wondered if the numbness from his legs might have spread, if some kind of an infection had boiled up to his brain to spawn hallucinations. But the enlarged shadow was only the press bus roaring past on its way to the finish. The crowds were so thick on Commonwealth Avenue that the truck had to follow the same line as the runners.

For a long time, the truck hung behind him, a distraction, a rumbling smelly thing grinding on his shoulder. He glanced up and saw a blur of faces and camera nozzles pointed down at him. Well, go ahead past, dammit. But it couldn't because of the crowd. The driver inched along behind him, and when he finally goosed the truck to move past, the rearview mirror clipped Beardsley on the shoulder. Not enough to knock him off stride, but enough to piss him off so that he snarled and punched the bus in frustration.

Then the truck was gone. Dick had just returned to his rhythm when, a half mile farther, a disheveled-looking man emerged from the crowd and reached out to him. At first, he thought the man was offering water. Beardsley shook his head, but the man kept coming. There was a wild glint to his eye, his right arm was outstretched, and if Dick had any strength left, he would have been terrified. The man carried something in his hand. But, thank God, it wasn't a gun or other weapon. It was money, a wad of folded greenbacks. The fellow tried to shove the bills into the elastic of Beardsley's shorts. It seemed to Dick that the man, while clearly deranged, was somehow in tune with a dark, unacknowledged theme of the day. Beardsley shoved him aside. Then the man tried to stuff the cash down Salazar's shorts. The cops finally grabbed him and dragged him away.

By the 25th mile, Beardsley didn't need to look for the shadow anymore. They had been running together their whole lives. He felt Salazar's presence more palpably than he did his own ruined legs. My God, he thought, one more mile and I'm going to win this thing.

Continuing to move in a disembodied, dreamlike cloud, Beardsley flashed on his father. For his 16th birthday present, his father had given him that IOU plane ticket, good one day for a trip to the Boston Marathon. Dick recalled a photograph of his parents taken just after they got married. They looked so happy then and full of hope. People said he was a dead ringer for his father when he'd been a younger man. Now it was tougher to see the resemblance because his father had developed a big gut. He was skinny everywhere else, but he had this enormous, hard belly that he let kids punch for fun.

Other, darker memories surfaced: One day when Dick was 12, his father was home in the afternoon, off from his salesman's job. It was one of his dad's good days—he had been drinking, of course, but only a few beers. Accompanied by Dick's best friend in grade school, Steve Thompson, the father and son took off on a fishing trip to a lake near Bemidji. As they approached Wayzata on the drive home, they stopped at a clearing in the woods so the boys could do some practice shooting. Bill Beardsley reached into the trunk of his car. He took out the 16-gauge shotgun that his own father had given him and, for the first time, handed it to Dick.

"Let's see what you can do with this thing," he said.

Wayzata was still a country town. Dick once brought down an 8-point buck less than a mile from the town center. His father set up some tin cans as targets and then walked over to the side of the field. He turned to Dick and nodded. Dick lifted the shotgun in a slow arc, and suddenly the quiet of the afternoon was split by a roar. His finger had slipped. He'd squeezed the trigger as the barrel of the shotgun was pointing straight at his father. Dick looked up in horror, but his father was still standing there. The shells couldn't have missed him by more than a few inches.

His father didn't say anything. He just walked over and took the shotgun and got back in the car. Dick and Steve climbed into the passenger seat. Nobody said a word. His father drove into town and straight to a tavern. He parked and got out, leaving the two boys in the car. His father went into the tavern and stayed there for a long time.

Now, as Beardsley traveled Boston's 25th mile, tears started to well up. Dick told himself to cut it out, get into this, attend to business.

If he was going to break away, it would have to be now because the red zone, the last quarter-mile, belonged to Alberto. Dick made no pretense of owning a killer finishing kick. He wasn't a closer. His chance had come on the hills. He had run them hard and well—exactly according to plan—but he still hadn't been able to escape the shadow. They were moving into Alberto country now.

But if Dick had not pulled away, neither had he been left behind. He remained in the lead. There was still work to do. He would have to summon one final surge. Salazar had said that he saw no runner at Boston worth his worry. *Well, worry about this, pal.*

Dick bore down. A shout of pain arose from his right hamstring. The leg that had felt like air suddenly turned to rubber. You could see the knotted muscle bulging.

Salazar blew past him. This was wrong on every conceivable level.

Then the motorcycle cops roared past, following Salazar, forming a phalanx around the new leader. The motorcycles massed together, and for the first time all day, Dick Beardsley lost sight of his opponent.

15

Alberto Salazar and his family arrived in Medjugorje for their 10-day pilgrimage in late June 1990. The family rented rooms in a private home, which turned out to be a surprisingly comfortable arrangement. In the 9 years since the Marian apparitions had propelled the town into the international tourist industry, its residents had grown expert in taking care of foreign visitors. And yet, the people of Medjugorje didn't come across as hardened, cynical, or dollar-hungry. Alberto could sense his hosts' authenticity and eagerness to share their faith. His father had been right, at least in the sense that a spiritual atmosphere enveloped the place. During their first few days in the village, however, Alberto and his family had experienced no hint of the miraculous. But he kept an open mind and remained vigilant. Along with his street clothes and rosary beads, he had packed his running gear.

Medjugorje seemed a world unto itself, an Oz-type kingdom. The village of 3,000 lay about 20 kilometers southeast of the provincial capital of Mostar, near the coast of the Adriatic, in the heart of Yugoslavia's Herzegovina region. Like most visitors from the West, especially Americans, Alberto knew or cared little about the Balkans' tangled geography, history, and politics. It was enough to know that the family was in Yugoslavia, which, though Communist, was the most open and democratic of the Eastern Bloc nations. It was rugged but handsome country, with a sunny Mediterranean climate reminiscent of coastal California. Forests of pine and oak covered the steep hills and ridges. The area's vineyards produced fine Zilavka and Blatina wines, while its fields yielded high-grade tobacco. To Salazar's mind, however, the village's honest, direct, peace-loving citizens formed its chief attribute. His natural, middle-class American skepticism quickly evaporated in the euphoric air. Pilgrims did not debate the veracity of the young seers, only how to interpret the divine messages they delivered. Medjugorje appeared to be a place with everything to share and nothing to hide.

By necessity, with hundreds of thousands of visitors pouring through town each year (a conservative estimate; some sources placed the annual number of visitors at around a million), the local priests had systematized the pilgrimage experience. First stop was Podbrdo Hill, or Apparition Hill, where, in 1981, the six children first encountered the apparition, the Gospa, the Holy Mother. There was a chapel on top of the hill, where visions and minor miracles were said to occur. Pilgrims who were physically able were encouraged to hike up nearby Mount Krizevac, where the chain on Alberto's father's rosary beads had purportedly turned gold. (Jose had repeated the story so often that Alberto knew it almost as well as the one about his father saving Castro's life: During his pilgrimage a few years earlier, Jose had climbed the mountain very slowly, in the company of his sister, stopping every few yards along the steep trail so the woman could catch her breath. When he reached the summit, he had removed the beads from his pocket. The silver-plated chain, Jose swore, had turned gold.)

After visiting Apparition Hill and the wooden crosses atop Mount Krizevac, pilgrims were directed to a large meadow, where priests in tents heard confession in five languages. Alberto found this sight especially inspiring—droves of earnest pilgrims queuing up to acknowledge their sins and seek forgiveness in the way that people in the secular world lined up for *Star Wars,* Disneyland, or some other empty entertainment. Each year, more confessions were heard in Medjugorje than any other parish in the world. During 1990, 1.9 million communions were served in the parish.

In the afternoon, the pilgrims ranged around town to meet the children—now young adults—who'd claimed to have been visited by the Gospa. This proceeded in as orderly and dignified a manner as possible, with the visitors again organized by language. At an appointed hour, the children fell into 10-minute-long trances, during which they were said to commune with the Holy Mother. When they came out of their trances, they relayed the Mother's message to a priest, who in turn communicated the teaching to the crowd of pilgrims in a choice of Slavic, French, German, Italian, or English.

"What struck me was God's presence in this obscure provincial village," Salazar said. "All of a sudden, I really believed. I just had this conviction that Our Lady was appearing."

A few days into the pilgrimage, Salazar was rewarded by what he reported to be a supernatural experience.

"Molly, the boys, and I all brought our own rosary beads from home," he explained. "We joked about them turning color like my father's. When we went to bed the first night, Molly and I put our beads on the dresser in our room. When we woke up the next morning, they hadn't changed, so I stopped thinking about it. But two mornings later when we got up and looked at our beads, they had changed from silver to gold. I couldn't believe it. I thought there was something about the air in the town that might have oxidized the metal. But that wasn't it—our boys' rosary beads hadn't changed at all. I was convinced this was the real deal."

Alberto was also moved by his visits with the young people who had experienced the apparitions. "There was no doubt that these kids had seen the Mother," Salazar insisted. "They were just normal kids, although all the attention they were getting didn't allow them anything close to a normal life. Still, they were amazingly patient and loving with everybody who came to them. There was no money in it for them. Their faith and love were genuine. A general blessing and peace radiated all through Medjugorje. The population was split between Christians and Muslims, but after the visitations, the town became unified."

Had Salazar ventured out of the official pilgrimage channels to the far side of Mount Krizevac, however, he might have formed a less enchanted opinion of the village. Beyond the mountain's wooden crosses, within a few kilometers of the center of Medjugorje, lay a village called Surmanci, which was bordered by a steep ravine. Here, on June 25, 1941, 40 years to the day before the Marian apparitions were first reported, agents of the Ustashe, a fascist Croat military group, had allegedly murdered 600 Serb civilians. Most of the victims were women and children. Evidence suggested that the Ustashe had pushed their victims off of a 75-foot-high cliff, then thrown hand grenades down after them.

The Surmanci massacre was just one episode in a 4-year reign of terror by the Ustashe, who openly collaborated with Hitler's occupying army, afflicting their traditional enemies, the Serbs, with a ferocity that apparently gave even the Gestapo pause. According to the Simon Wiesenthal Center, 1.8 million people died in Yugoslavia during World War II; 600,000 of the victims were Serbs. The Roman Catholic Croat Ustashe who besieged the Orthodox Christian Serbs were supported—according to some accounts, joined—by the Franciscan priests whose successors now presided over the purported Marian miracle. Instead of the disinterested, apolitical movement that was presented to the pilgrims, in other words, the Medjugorje phenomenon was in fact inextricably linked to the Balkans' violent history. The harmony that Salazar witnessed between the local Muslims and Roman Catholics, for instance, was in part due to the fact that the two groups had united to drive the Serbs from Herzegovina.

To be fair, Salazar and his fellow pilgrims would have had to take considerable pains to learn these unpleasant facts. Surmanci was not a stop on the pilgrimage tour. Indeed, Marshall Tito's Communist government was so determined to suppress the Surmanci story that officials had constructed a steel covering over the ravine. It was only in the mid-1990s, after the fall of Communism and the ensuing Balkan civil war, that the lid over Surmanci was finally lifted and the victims' bones exhumed and re-buried in a Serbian cemetery. By that time, of course, the Serbs were engaged in their own depredations against the Croats and Muslims, most prominently the terrible war crimes allegedly engi-neered by Slobodan Milosevic.

Medjugorje, in short, simmered in a murky stew of centuries-old hatred and violence, a fact which both the locals and tourists found convenient to ignore. The Vatican, for its part, didn't know what to do about the place. On the one hand, by the time of Alberto's visit, 30,000 priests and nuns from around the world had visited the site. The Medjugorje apparitions had energized the global Roman Catholic charismatic movement and inspired hun-dreds of thousands of confessions, communions, and conversions. On the other hand, Rome didn't control the action, which con-tinued to be run by the local Franciscan priests.

Back in 1981, just before the reported apparitions, the Franciscans engaged the Vatican-backed bishop of Mostar in a bitter turf battle over jurisdiction of the Medjugorje parish. Just as the bishop was about to gain control of the parish, the six children took their fateful June stroll up Podbrdo Hill. The Franciscan parish priest, Jozo Zovko, immediately embraced the children's story. The shrine's immediate, runaway popularity ended any chance that the bishop and the Vatican could assume control. A rather awkward but mutually profitable partnership ensued. The Franciscan-administered movement refrained from making any overtly political or anti-Vatican statements (according to the messages that the children reported, the Gospa was a strong supporter of the Pope). In return, the Vatican took an officially neutral position toward the apparitions. While refraining from granting Medjugorje the full-blown shrine status of Lourdes or Fatima, the church conceded that pilgrims journeyed to the village "in good faith." In fact, Pope John Paul II, a native Pole of strong pro-Marian, anti-Communist convictions, looked fondly upon Medjugorje. The Soviet-backed Yugoslavian government, for its part, at first tried to repress the movement, but soon let it alone. The rapidly fraying totalitarian state had much bigger worries.

Into this behind-the-looking-glass realm wandered the sickly, depressed, world-famous Cuban-American distance runner and his family. Like many pilgrims, Salazar arrived in the village seeking a resolution to an urgent personal dilemma. "For years, I had been praying every night for the Lord to heal me and allow me to run again," Salazar said. "Or if it was his will that I shouldn't run, for him to show me that clearly. I wanted to know. I wanted a sign, one way or the other."

Now it seemed that a sign was imminent. Alberto's rosary beads had turned gold. He felt the presence of the Holy Spirit in the six chosen children. Accepting the Gospa's teaching into his heart, Salazar rededicated himself to the church. He would no longer be a fair-weather Catholic, going through the motions of faith while in fact living for his own vanity. Now he would worship as the Gospa instructed, praying the rosary and mysteries throughout the day. He resolved to regularly attend Mass and confession. He would fast 2 days a week, as the Mother had instructed. He would no longer curse or indulge in anger. He would proclaim his faith to the world, witnessing for the Holy Mother.

On a practical level, Salazar resolved to go home and rid himself of his restaurant and its cocktail lounge. No more dealing booze to young people. He would sell the restaurant and take up Nike CEO Phil Knight's standing offer to go to work for the company in Portland. Finally, Alberto and Molly would conceive another child for the Gospa.

And in the light of this new life, the Lord would finally reveal Salazar's future as an athlete. A miracle might yet descend. Alberto would get it all back. The fine days of his prime would return.

Each day in Medjugorje, besides engaging in pilgrimage activities, Salazar would go for a run. There were few good trails in the area, so he stuck to the narrow roads that snaked through the hills. He ran past the hill where the Gospa had purportedly revealed herself to the Croat children and the hill from which the Ustashe had allegedly pitched Serb babies into the ravine. One morning, Alberto was out running when a car came barreling toward him.

He ran along the road toward the neighboring village of Ljubuski, a narrow, skanky road through the green hills, like Sonoma or Monterey but different, too. This country was old and hard with a strange taste to the air, a commingled stink and aroma of diesel fuel and wood smoke and dense, rich, peasant cooking. Alberto ran, thinking through the enormous changes tipping inside of him, the Holy Mother enveloping these crazy, blessed hills.

When a black car blasted up behind him on the narrow road, Alberto could feel the suck of wind. At the final instant, he glanced back. There was the car, like Dick Beardsley in the last yards at Boston. Alberto dove into the ditch at the side of the road, tumbling in the thorny underbrush, as the car from hell careened toward Ljubuski.

A few days later, Father Slavko Barbaric, a Franciscan priest in Medjugorge, conducted an interview with Salazar that was later published in a newsletter for the shrine. The runner began by recounting the episode with the car and the ditch.

"I didn't shout a single curse word at that driver," Salazar told the priest. "For me, that was a bigger accomplishment than winning a marathon."

Alberto then delved into what he regarded as his sinful past. He explained to Barbaric that he was once presented with a laurel wreath after winning a marathon. A few months later, when he removed the wreath from storage, he saw that the wreath had withered. Salazar now recognized this as an omen.

"Running isn't simply a discipline," he said. "It can become a compulsion—it can become like a god. If you worship this god, you forget everything else. And when you lose this god, you've got nothing."

Salazar made further revelations to Father Barbaric, who had trained as a psychiatrist in his native Germany and whose sudden death from a heart attack a few years later caused his followers to petition the Vatican for his beatification. Alberto, who for so long had shunned media interviews, poured out his heart to the priest. More than responding to Barbaric's questions, he seemed to be confessing out of his own desperate need.

When Father Barbaric quietly asked if he had more to confess. Salazar nodded.

"I was completely intolerant of others," he went on. "When you want to be first—when you need to be first—that attitude spills over into everything else in your life. I talked behind people's backs. I spoke hurtful words to my friends and family. If I didn't feel sociable, I just ignored people—or I behaved like such a jerk that they wished I had ignored them. If my employees at the restaurant didn't do exactly what I told them, I would rip them unmercifully. I was always fighting with someone. I used filthy language.

"But once I decided to come to Medjugorge, my life changed," Salazar went on. "All of my evil habits just disappeared, as if by a miracle. It happened when I went to confession, just before leaving the United States. I felt free," Alberto confessed, "I felt cleansed."

The deal was done, the message vouchsafed, the miracle procured. God had cast him out to sea and now, certainly, would deliver him to the far shore. Salazar was again blessed and favored. He would run as strongly as before—perhaps more brilliantly than before. Alberto would no longer run for himself, however, but for the glory of God and thus bring others to Him. He would put his gift to use. That had been the plan all along, but Alberto had been too blind to see it. Now the light would flood down and all the beads turn gold.

Salazar made good on his vows. He flew home to Eugene, sold his restaurant, moved the family to Portland, and went to work for Nike. He recited the rosary while driving Portland's freeways and running the trails through the city's Forest Park. He attended Mass and confession and fasted on Tuesday and Friday. He worked at Nike's gleaming Beaverton campus, where a building had been named in his honor. Alberto had enlisted all the powers of heaven and earth in order to run like himself again.

He prayed and waited, but, to Salazar's crushing disappointment, deliverance never arrived. After the familiar burst of initial improvement, his daily run became the same gray, dispiriting, uphill slog as before his pilgrimage. Despite the fact that he'd given himself over to the Gospa and done her bidding—followed the Mother's instructions exactly—his depression returned.

Driving the freeway, doggedly mumbling the rosary, he again found himself staring at the onrushing traffic. He did not want that semi to drift across the median strip and plow into him. He did not want to die, but if God should so order it, would it really be such a tragedy? What else was left? He had gone to the Balkans and watched silver turn gold. He had been saved by direct intervention of the Holy Mother. He had a healthy and beautiful family, a million dollars in the bank, and a fine house in the West Hills with a commanding view of downtown Portland. The coolest company in the world had named a building after him. Yet all of this wasn't enough. For all of his extravagant blessings, Alberto still wasn't as happy or fulfilled as the guy driving the forklift in the Nike warehouse, whose prayers extended only to a plea for good snowboarding or that his girlfriend might wear that lacy little black thing she bought last weekend at the mall.

Alberto Salazar still couldn't run. Even more painfully, God had not revealed to him that he should stop running.

16

Just when Beardsley thought nothing more could possibly go wrong, something did. A moment after losing sight of Salazar, with less than a mile to go, he stepped in a pothole. The misstep occurred directly in front of the Eliot Lounge, the celebrated Kenmore Square saloon where Tommy Leonard—the Boston Marathon's unofficial greeter—tended bar and photographs of Rodgers, Johnny Kelley, Jock Semple, Joan Benoit, Clarence DeMar, Tarzan Brown, and other marathon legends looked down from the walls. It now seemed certain that Salazar's photo was about to join them.

With his impeccable Greater Boston Track Club-University of Oregon-Nike-2:08:13 pedigree, Salazar had at last seized the lead, which seemed his rightful place. It was as if cartoon-time had passed and the grown-ups had come back into the room. And yet, Beardsley, with his tacky little South Dakota State-Grandma's Marathon-New Balance-Rush City résumé, had won over the big-city crowd. Maybe it was Dick's jaunty painter's cap or the fact that he worked with Bill Squires, who was about as Boston as Paul Revere. Beardsley's skinny, pale, boy-next-door demeanor might have been a factor. Certainly, the crowd reacted favorably to his desire and desperation. Beardsley was running the Boston Marathon as if it were the final race of his life, and he was forcing Salazar to do the same. The crowd roared as Beardsley ran past.

But now the race seemed over. His opponent's shadow had vanished from the asphalt. This was the point where Dick could honorably fold his tents. Nobody would think the less of him for it. Sooner or later, every runner gave up against Salazar and started running for second place. But that wasn't right, Beardsley thought. Alberto was only human; like every other runner on the course, he had a weakness to hide. If nothing else over the last 26 miles, Dick had proved that fact.

He'd stepped in a pothole, and that ripped it up completely. The best he could do now was crawl in. What if the next runner trailing passed him? After all this work and heartache, he might not even get second place. He had an awful nightmare vision of the whole field passing him. All 6,000-plus runners who had parted like the Red Sea for him a lifetime ago back in Hopkinton, each one of them streaming past as he crawled on his hands and knees and finally his belly toward a finish line that kept receding as runner after runner blew past him until they were all gone. Not even Coach Squires waited at the finish line to lift him up.

Beardsley braced for the fall. He tensed every muscle against the electric bolt of pain that would certainly cripple him now that he'd stepped in the pothole. Amazingly, providentially, no pain arose. Dick looked down. The muscle knot had dissolved. For an instant, he thought he might have fainted. Perhaps he was dreaming. But no, there were his feet and legs turning over, and there was the crowd pressing all around. And up ahead, just barely visible in front of the flotilla of motorcycle cops, grim and white-faced, wearing his salt-rimmed red-banded Athletics West singlet, Alberto Salazar blasted toward the finish. Beardsley put his head down and started to sprint.

17

One summer morning in 1993, Alberto Salazar picked up the telephone to receive a call from an acquaintance, Dr. Paul Raether, who had momentous news to share concerning the two men's mutual, long-suffered affliction.

Raether's problems had started in 1981, when he was in his late twenties and finishing his residency in physiatry (a relatively little-known specialty that essentially takes an MD's approach to physical therapy) at the University of Minnesota Medical School. By avocation, Raether was one of those 2:30 marathoners who were relatively common at the time—accomplished citizen-runners who finished among the top 100 each year at the Boston Marathon. One weekend, Raether ran a 15-kilometer road race in 44:53, a near-national-class time. The next day, he went out for an easy recovery run, aiming for nothing more than to flush the lactic acid out of his stiff leg muscles. His easy run, however, took off in unexpected directions. Elated by his previous day's effort, Raether ended up running twice as long and hard as he'd intended.

That night, a tickle rose in his throat. By bedtime, he couldn't swallow and a fever bloomed. For the next week, he drank a lot of water and dosed up on vitamin C. He returned to work and forced himself to jog a few miles each day; the common wisdom held that if you could run yourself into a bad cold, you could run yourself out of one, too. But while the viral infection abated enough for Raether to work and perform normal activities, it would not allow him to run at a fraction of his normal intensity.

Days, weeks, and then months passed with no discernable progress. Every time he tried to run, his body failed to respond. Once a source of sharp pleasure, running became a vexing, frustrating, bewildering chore. He consulted his colleagues and pored over the sports medicine literature, to no avail. As time went by, he turned more of his attention to his profession and family. The months slipped into a year and then another. Raether was never quite sick, nor was he depressed, but he missed that incomparable jolt of vitality that hard running could yield. He kept up with the research pertinent to his malaise, hoping for a breakthrough, but his sport seemed like a coin shining at the bottom of an increasingly murky pool.

Finally, 12 years later, in 1993, Raether had come across a paper concerning a new drug and its effect on brain chemistry. The study presented a litany of breakthroughs, with side effects so negligible that Raether had to read it again to make sure he'd gotten it right. At the end of his second reading, he phoned his treating physician and asked him to prescribe the medicine for his condition.

Raether filled the prescription, swallowed the first dose of pills, then put the matter out of his mind. The medication typically took 2 to 3 weeks to show results. But the next morning, as he saw patients in his office at the Kaiser Sunnyside Medical Center in Clackamas, Oregon, Raether felt a tingling sensation in his legs. He tried to remain calm and objective. His pulse and blood pressure were unchanged, and his mental processes appeared unaltered. But the tingling, electric feeling intensified through the morning. As he moved through his rounds, Raether had to consciously suppress the bounce in his step. By midday, there was no denying the fact that his legs felt more alive than they had in a dozen years. He went out at lunchtime and ran hard for the first time since his ill-fated "recovery" run in 1981.

Raether finished his workout and went straight to a telephone. He had met Alberto Salazar 2 years earlier at a track meet in Eugene, where they had struck up a conversation based on their mutual love for running and the remarkably similar maladies that kept them from it. Salazar had never been Raether's patient, but since that meeting, they had kept in touch. When Salazar answered the phone, Raether got right to the point.

"Alberto," he said, "have you ever tried Prozac?"

Salazar was now 35 years old. As was the case with Raether, 12 years had passed since the onset of his condition, and, also like the physician, he had begun to reconcile himself to his state. He enjoyed his job with Nike, working as a liaison to the company's elite track-and-field athletes. He'd also begun to dabble in coaching, directing the training of the star middle-distance runner Mary Decker Slaney, who lived in Eugene. Salazar's sons were embarked on their own promising athletic careers, and his daughter, Maria, was now 2 years old.

In 1992, Salazar had taken a second pilgrimage to Medjugorje. He found the town more crowded than on his first visit, with a much more developed tourist industry, but emanating the same aura of simplicity and grace. He returned to the United States even more firmly grounded in his faith. Alberto continued to try to live by the Gospa's dictates, praying throughout the day, fasting on Tuesdays and Fridays, regularly attending Mass and confession. He strove to be patient, open, forgiving, and magnanimous. His depression lingered, although not as severely as before. On most days, Salazar could accept that he was destined to live in an attenuated, twilight state between illness and good health. He continued to try to run because running remained his calling.

Through his job with Nike, meanwhile, he vicariously experienced the triumphs and setbacks of his fellow elite athletes. At the Barcelona Olympics in 1992, for instance, it was Salazar's duty to drive the American sprinter Michael Johnson away from the stadium after Johnson's shocking failure to qualify for the finals in the 200 meters. A case of food poisoning had deprived Johnson, the world-record holder in the event, of a seemingly certain gold medal (at the Atlanta Olympics 4 years later, Johnson would win gold in both the 200 and 400). No one could better empathize with the devastated sprinter than Salazar.

Somewhat anticlimactically, physicians had at long last determined that Alberto suffered from a severe case of exercise-induced asthma. Tests showed that his lung function was only 60 percent that of a normal person's (an elite runner's lung capacity was typically 125 percent of normal). The condition had almost certainly developed in response to Salazar's severe overheating at the 1982 Boston Marathon. The trauma of that marathon had also compromised the workings of his hypothalamus, the section of the brain that regulates body temperature. While there was solace in knowing what ailed him, there seemed little, at this late date, that Salazar could do about it.

Until now, when Raether called with his potentially bombshell news about Prozac. A serotonin reuptake inhibitor—a revolutionary type of bioengineered, psychoactive drug—Prozac had been introduced to the American public in 1987, and in 1993 rang up $1.2 billion in sales. Prozac, however, was classified as a sedative rather than a stimulant. Salazar wondered how the trendy antidepressant could possibly help an athlete, especially a former world-class marathoner with a sputtering hypothalamus, misfiring glands, and lungs operating at only half-capacity.

Raether hypothesized that Prozac alleviated his symptoms and might help Salazar's because the drug corrected the brain's cortical-enzyme levels. Under the stress of fighting a battle or running a marathon, Raether explained, an individual's normal cortical-enzyme level of 10 is pushed up to 15 or 20. Following the ordeal, the enzyme levels return to normal. But chronically stressful situations—prolonged combat or, in the case of Salazar and Raether, prolonged overtraining—produce chronically high cortical-enzyme levels. Following an ordeal, the individual's levels remain elevated. As a result, when the overstressed soldier or marathoner encounters yet another challenge, he can't produce additional cortical enzymes in response. He becomes like a bus grinding up a steep hill, stuck in low gear. Apparently, Prozac had reset Raether's cortical-enzyme response mechanism so it functioned properly, freeing him, after 12 sputtering years, to finally engage all of his gears.

Salazar listened to Raether with the same sense of astonishment and excitement with which, years earlier, he had first read the Medjugorje tracts that his father had sent him. Another shot was arcing toward him from deep left field. A few years earlier, of course Alberto would have leaped at the opportunity to try the latest, highly touted "cure." But now he hesitated, praying over the decision of whether or not to take Prozac. He did not pray for an answer—he had stopped expecting angels or miracles—but for the ability to think clearly.

Prozac certainly sounded fascinating, and Raether was trustworthy. His explanation about the drug's effects sounded plausible. Most intriguing was the fact that Raether, whose malaise was so similar to Alberto's, could run again. Prozac, moreover, did not appear on the International Amateur Athletic Federation's list of banned substances.

On the other hand, the physician's suggestion seemed far-fetched, almost desperate. Prozac was generally conceived as a medication for depressed housewives and salesmen seeking an extroverted edge, not for professional athletes. Studies indicated that, for healthy subjects, Prozac actually compromised athletic performance. At great cost, moreover, Alberto was just getting used to the fact that he would never run well again. The overwhelming likelihood was that the same thing would happen with Prozac as had happened with sleep therapy, hormonal therapy, training in Kenya, and, for that matter, the Holy Mother: skyrocketing hopes and a day or two of mildly improved running, followed by a severe letdown and crash. By bitter experience, he had learned that each new crash hurt a little worse than the one before.

On balance, however, Alberto decided that taking Prozac was worth the risk. He couldn't see how his performance could be "compromised" more than was already the case. Some people might laugh, or worse, when they found out he was taking Prozac, but what did that matter? Since Salazar had begun to publicly witness about his experiences in Medjugorje, some people wrote him off as a crank anyway.

So Alberto called his doctor, obtained a prescription, and became another one of the six million Americans taking this widely used prescription medicine. The results were spectacular. Three days later, he could run again.

"I was ecstatic," Salazar said. "I was shocked. Paul had turned me on to a magic pill. Before Prozac, the fastest pace I could run was about 5:20 per mile, and even doing that killed me. Three days after I began taking Prozac, I ran a workout of three 1-mile repeats. I ran each of them in 5 minutes, comfortably. A few days later, I did a 6-by-1-mile workout at 4:42 per mile."

The drug also had an unintended, more far-reaching effect. "I had already made my second trip to Medjugorje, but I still felt sad, like nothing really seemed worth doing," Salazar explained. "Looking back, it seems obvious that I was clinically depressed. The truth is that depression and mental illness run on both sides of my family. When I was running well, my obsession absorbed my depression. But now that I wasn't winning races and constantly getting faster, the depression had all the room in the world to grow. Instead of making me happy, running made me miserable. I never told my doctor about this—he prescribed Prozac for my glandular imbalance. But as soon as I started taking it, I felt amazingly better. I stopped having death fantasies. It was like I didn't really know how bad I had felt until I started feeling good."

Although unaware of it, Salazar had responded in textbook fashion to the antidepressant. "Prozac often surprises us," Peter D. Kramer wrote in his 1993 bestseller, *Listening to Prozac*. "Sometimes it will change only one trait in the person under treatment, but often it goes far beyond a single intended effect. You take it to treat a symptom, and it transforms your sense of self. . . . The medical ethicists approach Prozac as if it were a case of dull or bright, down or up. Unlike amphetamine, Prozac is not a case of down or up but of same or other. Prozac has the power to transform the whole person—illness and temperament. When you take it, you risk widespread change."

"I believe that God guided me to keep the faith through all the years because the answer—in my case, Prozac—would be coming," Salazar said. "When my Prozac use became public, I drew a lot of flak. Some people assumed I was doping, and others criticized me because I was talking about my religion on the one hand and taking an antidepressant on the other. As if the two were mutually exclusive. My parish priest takes Prozac. It's got nothing to do with faith."

Nevertheless, the news that the legendary former world-record holder in the marathon was taking an antidepressant spread quickly—and often inaccurately—through the international running community. "His 15th-place showing in the 1984 Los Angeles Olympic Games had taken away Alberto Salazar's taste for running," began one article. "The three-time winner of the New York Marathon and world running star was at the end of his tether. His body was no longer responding. His immune system was giving out on him. Even routine jogging with his colleagues at Nike Inc., in Oregon was a torment. He consulted 'all the doctors' to no avail—until that day in the summer of 1993 when Paul Raether, a marathon runner and doctor, told him about the antidepressant. After Salazar's comeback, a number of runners at all levels, depressed or not, went on Prozac."

Now, instead of provoking sympathy, Salazar's case aroused suspicious sneers and smirks. In 1994, for instance, he was a member of a team of Nike runners that won the Hood to Coast Relay in Oregon. Afterward, adidas team members sardonically displayed bumper stickers on their cars reading, "We run without Prozac." The barb, while aimed at Salazar, also poked fun at the "Prozac Nation" popularity of the drug.

If he had been caught taking performance-boosting steroids or erythropoietin (EPO), ironically, the response might have been more positive. Those substances, while illegal, were much better understood in elite athletes' circles. Prozac, by contrast, treated conditions—depression, anxiety, shyness, insecurity—that athletes were loath to acknowledge. Among prominent professional athletes, only Julie Krone, a thoroughbred jockey, had talked freely about her depression and concomitant use of Prozac-class drugs.

When questioned by the media about his use of the drug, Salazar talked only about hormonal imbalances and asthma, not his near-suicidal depression and the history of mental illness in his family. At the same time, he neither denied Prozac nor apologized for taking it. Salazar had displayed a similar independence of thought during his spiritual journey. Professional sports teemed with born-again athletes, ballplayers, and others who subscribed to evangelical Christianity. A second baseman interviewed on national TV after hitting a game-winning home run could point to the sky and thank Jesus, and no one would raise an eyebrow. But it took considerable courage for Salazar—who was so conservative, so concerned with propriety, so deeply steeped in Latin, athletic, and corporate machismo—to step dramatically out of the mainstream by embracing the Virgin Mary with one hand and Prozac with the other. After a lifetime of obsessing on traditional manly virtue, perhaps, Salazar was ready to indulge the more feminine side of his nature. Or perhaps, after all that he'd endured, he simply didn't care what his critics thought.

"The use I made of Prozac has nothing to do with my athletic career, but with my health," he insisted.

Alberto could run again—up to a point. Although Prozac had apparently righted his cortical-enzyme levels, it couldn't reverse the damage that asthma had caused his lungs, which still functioned at only half the normal capacity. At age 35, moreover, Salazar had inched past his physical prime. Even with fully functioning lungs, he would no longer be capable of competing on a world-class level in the 10,000 meters or marathon. His ability to withstand pain, however, remained undiminished—and unparalleled. Salazar could no longer run indefinitely at a 5-minute-per-mile pace, but he could do so at 6 minutes per mile. More important, he was convinced that God had restored his running—at whatever speed—for a purpose. So Alberto Salazar took yet another iconoclastic step. He turned to ultramarathons.

18

On the morning of October 1, 1996, Dick Beardsley flipped through his notebook—the one in which he ostensibly recorded bait purchases but in fact tracked his drug buys—and saw that it was time to return to Moorhead and hit up the pharmacy at Wal-Mart, in the mall where he'd first forged prescriptions 10 weeks earlier.

When Mary asked him about his plans for the day, he made up some story about driving to Fargo on one pretext or another. She vaguely nodded. It didn't really matter anymore what Dick said or what Mary believed, or pretended to believe. He assumed that on some level she knew what was going on—several times over the last few years she had brought up the topic of addiction, but he'd always put her off. Perhaps at this point, Mary knew exactly what he was up to but no longer really cared.

Beardsley's faltering marriage was one more thing he'd have to set right later. Drug addiction, he had discovered, was all about priorities. Pills invariably formed the organizing principle. You arranged your day around pills and everything else—including family—fell into place around them. In this respect the addict's life so closely resembled the professional runner's life that Dick would at times experience a fleeting shot of shame. In general, however, he was too busy feeding his addiction to feel guilty about it.

Beardsley drove west on Highway 10 to Moorhead, a route so familiar that he barely noticed the landscape, which was passing into autumn. The tips of the maple and elm leaves were already curling and turning color. Fall always made him think of Lake Chisago and Bloom Lake Farm. Come November, it would be 7 years since the PTO accident and that first glorious shot of Demerol at the small hospital in Chisago City.

Although the active phase of Beardsley's addiction began at the time of his first accident, the seeds of his disease had most likely been planted at birth. Both of his parents had been alcoholics, his father publicly and his mother privately. As a younger man, Beardsley's father drank beer openly and steadily through the day, and in middle age did the same with gin. Dick rarely saw his father either blatantly drunk or unequivocally sober. His mother, by contrast, hid her bottles around the house, logging most of her intake while her children were at school. Carole Ross, for example, never suspected that Dick's mother was a drunk until she phoned the Beardsley house once in the middle of the day and found her babbling and incoherent. Seared by his parents' mutual illness, Dick had fled from any sort of intoxicant.

But if both of your parents are alcoholics, Beardsley would soon learn, there's an 80 percent chance that, at some point in your life, you will get hooked on one substance or another. No matter how careful or abstemious you might be, 8 chances in 10 you will fall prey to fate. One cold, dark morning with snow on the way, you will be rushing around like a fool, skipping breakfast and hollering at your wife because she forgot to bring the hay down for the cows, and while loading corn in the grain elevator your pants leg will catch in the PTO U-joint. You will get slammed around in terrible circles. They will take you away in an ambulance, and in the hospital they will annul your pain with a class of wonder drugs called opioids, which will hit your genetically primed brain cells the way a smoldering cigarette butt hits the tinder-dry underbrush of a California canyon in early September.

From that day forward, consciously or unconsciously, actively or dormantly, you will devote yourself to recapturing the rush of that first transcendent hit. Simultaneously, you will deny that you are condemned to this futile pursuit. Eventually, you will either overcome your denial and recover from your craving, or else you will die from it.

Dick covered the 40 miles to Moorhead in a prudent 50 minutes, driving with extreme caution so he wouldn't get pulled over. He had taken to concealing his pills in a box he had tucked under his truck's dashboard. Since his buzz—or, more accurately, his suspension of pain—barely lasted a half hour now, he would have to dose up at some point during the morning's mission.

He turned into the Wal-Mart lot, parked in his favorite spot, and dashed off three bogus prescriptions, one each for Demerol, Percocet, and Valium. He climbed out of his pickup and walked across the lot to the store. He'd made this trip scores of times over the last several years, bearing both legitimate and faked prescriptions—although Beardsley, in classic addict fashion, no longer made a distinction between the two. He moved through the automatic doors and into the blaring yet comforting universe of Wal-Mart, then proceeded directly to the pharmacy, where he was pleased to find George behind the counter. George was Dick's favorite pharmacist. The two men had fished together several times. They always joked around when Beardsley came in for his pills.

"George, how the heck are you?"

George did not look up. For what seemed like a very long time, he kept staring down at the pharmacy counter. Dick went cold.

When George finally lifted his eyes, they were flat and dead and would not meet Beardsley's. Dick felt the blood leave his face. He knew immediately that it was over.

The druggist came around the counter, put his hand on Dick's shoulder, and led him down an empty shopping aisle. He quietly explained that the doctor had called the day before with the shocking news that Dick had been forging prescriptions—a great many prescriptions. The doctor was phoning all the pharmacies on Beardsley's circuit to warn them that, as certain as Detroit Lake would freeze over in January, Dick would soon return to one of them for more pills.

"I prayed that you wouldn't pick Wal-Mart," George said with a haggard smile, "but apparently God had already set your schedule."

Instead of panic, Beardsley felt an enormous surge of relief. "George," he said, "I need help."

From the pharmacy office, Beardsley called the doctor's office and made an appointment for 4:30 that afternoon. After hanging up the phone, Dick turned to the druggist. Now what? Would George be required to call the police? Had the time come for handcuffs and patrol cars? But George merely shook his hand and wished him good luck. Moments later, Dick was standing by his truck in the morning sunshine. The whole thing had taken only a few minutes. What would happen, he wondered, if he simply drove over to Kmart and wrote another prescription?

But the rhythm and pitch of the traffic on Highway 10 seemed altered. The light on the parking lot had changed. Dick felt as if he'd aged 20 years in a few minutes, yet at the same time he felt lightened and shrived. There was a vial full of pills stashed under the dashboard of his pickup. He knew he ought to gobble the pills in the preemptive manner that he'd chugged water all through the

'82 Boston Marathon; very soon, he knew, every cell in his body would be screaming out for opioids. Yet for some reason, Beardsley lacked any appetite for pills.

He drove home in a floating, limbolike cloud. There was a certain exhilaration to getting caught, which temporarily eclipsed his panic. This grace period, he knew, would pass quickly. The first job was to tell Mary. For years, he had devotedly nurtured and jealously guarded his addiction; the prospect of sharing his secret with another person—even his wife—was unsettling. But the talk went better than he had any right to expect. Mary maintained her composure, which was almost worse than if she'd screamed and thrown things. Dick assumed that that stage would come later. To his great relief, she said she wouldn't leave him.

The adrenaline rush of getting caught carried him through the next several hours, which he spent meeting a few work commitments, gearing up for the afternoon drive to Fargo, and then making the drive itself. He hadn't taken a pill since 7:30 that morning, the longest he'd gone without painkillers for years. His head hurt, but thus far the distress was manageable. The elation accompanying his new state buoyed him. On the other hand, his cover had been blown, his secret identity exposed to the light. What could he call himself now?

The receptionist at the clinic in Fargo treated him with deference, showing Beardsley right in to see the doctor. Ironically, it was much faster service than all the times he'd come here faking pain to cop pills. The orthopedist, for his part, greeted Beardsley as if this were just another routine appointment. He assured Dick that he wanted to help him. He wasn't angry, he said, just disappointed.

Dick hung his head. Disappointment, letting people down, the whole guilt trip—he knew how to play this scene. He didn't need to fake it.

"Unfortunately . . . ," the doctor said, and Dick looked up desolately. After giving you the good news, if there was any, doctors always seemed to begin their next sentence with that word. " . . . because the forgeries were under my name, the drug enforcement officers are obliged to investigate. They need to make sure I wasn't mixed up in all this. In fact," the doctor's voice took on an edge, "there happen to be two gentlemen from the DEA waiting to talk to us in the next room."

With that news, the exaltation of getting caught—the sense of election it invoked—summarily dissolved. Dick's composure melted faster than a sheen of morning ice in the May sunshine. Two agents with the Federal Drug Enforcement Agency, in crisp, dark suits, entered the office. They flashed their badges and shook Dick's hand with firm grips. The officers emanated an aura of the outside world, an unpitying world of courtrooms and prison blocks. Beardsley started to weep as the agents took seats facing him.

"Dick," one of them began, speaking in the same fatherly tone as the doctor, "I'm afraid we've got a problem with the number of prescriptions you've written over the last several months. We're looking at 1,500 pills in the month of August alone." The agent moved his chair closer. "We're thinking that maybe you didn't take all those pills yourself? That maybe you sold a few to some of your friends?"

Now Dick panicked. "No!" he wailed. "Every one of those pills went straight down my throat!"

Beardsley wept louder. Even in the midst of his terror, however, he felt a perverse surge of pride: Veteran federal drug-enforcement agents could not believe that one person had taken all those pills. Apparently, Dick really had been the finest dope addict around.

Over the next hour, Beardsley told the agents everything. He summarized the farm accident and his introduction to painkillers, then in detail described his activities since July. He explained how he practiced his craft, leading the agents out to his truck to show them his X-Acto knife, glue, and ruler. He displayed his notebook, and translated the code he employed to mask and track his illicit inventory. He showed them the cache of pills underneath the dashboard. If the agents had asked, he would have demonstrated how he gulped the pills down dry. They didn't ask. Beardsley eyed his pill box wistfully.

From the doctor's office, the agents delivered him to a hospital in Fargo. The hospital lacked a detox unit, so he was admitted into the psychiatric ward. If any wisps of euphoria were still lingering, they now evaporated. Beardsley's adrenal glands were tapped out. He hadn't had a fix for 12 hours. He had a crushing headache, and the nurses wouldn't give him anything for it. Hospital staffers kept coming in to draw blood and take his blood pressure and push forms in front of him to sign. His headache intensified. He began to comprehend the gravity of his predicament. He realized he had dragged Mary and Andy down, too. Dick's head felt like it was splitting open, and all he had for relief was a damp washcloth. Finally, in the middle of the night, the nurses gave him some Percocet and Demerol. The headache eased. For a few hours, he was able to sleep.

Beardsley spent 9 days in the Fargo hospital, during which he was weaned off of painkillers and started on methadone. He learned the ropes of rehab and took his first baby steps on the interminable trek through 12-step country. Since its investigation confirmed Beardsley's assertion that he hadn't been dealing pills, the DEA declined to prosecute him. The doctor also refrained from pressing charges. The county district attorney, however, citing the volume of drugs that Beardsley had illegally acquired, did choose to prosecute.

In early December, the first reporter caught wind of the affair, and within days the story went national. Articles appeared in the *New York Times, USA Today,* and the national running media. Every large newspaper, TV station, and radio station in the Upper Midwest sent reporters to Detroit Lakes to tell how Dick Beardsley—the fourth-fastest American marathoner of all time, the squeaky-clean dairy farmer and inspirational speaker who had heroically battled Alberto Salazar at the 1982 Boston Marathon— had descended into the depths of felony drug addiction.

"When the story hit the media, I was just devastated," Beardsley said. "It was the lowest point I had ever been. Beyond the embarrassment and shame I had brought upon Mary and Andy, I felt like I had let down everybody who had ever watched me run or listened to me speak. I had portrayed myself as a certain kind of person—this innocent, boyish character—when I had really been somebody else. But at the same time, I really was that innocent character, too. I couldn't understand it myself—and I couldn't imagine that anybody else would. Thank goodness, I was wrong."

Mary and Andy stood by him, as did his friends in Detroit Lakes and around the country. On March 28, 1997, Dick Beardsley was convicted of forgery and felony possession of a controlled substance. He was sentenced to 240 hours of community service work, 5 years' probation, and a $1,000 fine that the judge later replaced with 200 additional hours of community service. Beardsley had faced a maximum sentence of 5 years in prison and a $10,000 fine.

"From the moment I got caught, I cooperated completely with the authorities," he said. "I admitted everything. That helped when it came time for sentencing. And of course it helped that I had achieved some fame as an athlete—that holds a lot of water, especially here in Minnesota. Everybody remembered the guy from Wayzata who ran against Salazar at the '82 Boston Marathon. I had lots of people vouching for me. All those things worked in my favor with the judge. But the truth was I was just as much a criminal as any poor guy doing mandatory prison time for buying crack or heroin on the street."

As was the case after Beardsley's farm accident, the national running community sent money and other forms of support. From Boston, Bill Squires mailed Dick a check for $1,000, along with a note of encouragement. "You've overcome worse than this, Dickie," the coach wrote. "Just pretend like it's Heartbreak Hill."

Through the winter's long, sober, often sleepless nights, Beardsley had time to reflect on the '82 Boston Marathon. He had been telling the story of the race to audiences for years; it formed his most popular set piece. In the narrative, Alberto always played the role of arrogant, overconfident champion, and Dick the role of plucky underdog working against overwhelming odds. Now he wondered if that version was accurate. In the same way that Beardsley was both farm boy and dope fiend, couldn't the Boston Marathon also have a double meaning, a hidden narrative? Could it be possible, for instance, that Alberto, and not Dick, had been the true underdog?

After all, Beardsley had prepped for Boston with 3 months of withering, laser-intense training. The marathon fell at the absolute zenith of his career. The course and the weather had been ideally suited to his talents. Most important, Dick had run the Boston Marathon with nothing to lose and no real thought for tomorrow. That gave him an incalculable advantage over Salazar.

"You better be careful, Dick," his friend and fellow elite runner Garry Bjorklund had once warned him. "You're playing with fire by running so many fast marathons. The body's not designed for that kind of stress. Sooner or later you're going to have to pay a price."

Beardsley began to pay that price the moment he finished the Boston Marathon. Indeed, his bill started to come due as he flew down Heartbreak Hill and the feeling left his legs. Even at that moment, he realized he was drawing down capital that could never be replenished. He knew he would never run that well again.

"I was in the lead in the greatest race in the world, in front of the greatest runner in the world," he said. "It was almost too much for me to take in. And it was certainly too much for my body and mind to recover from. After Boston, my brain told me, 'No más.' When you push yourself to your limit, your absolute limit, and then go beyond that limit, your brain finally says, 'Huh-uh, we're not going back there again. You had your shot, buddy.'"

So in a way, Salazar had walked into an ambush. With unwitting but devastating effectiveness, Dick had sandbagged the world's greatest distance runner. If Alberto had had any inkling of what lay in store, he could have backed out of the Boston Marathon. He could have honestly said that his hamstring was hurting and he couldn't compete. Then Boston wouldn't have permanently damaged him. He would have gone on to win an Olympic gold medal—several of them, probably—and set more world records. Or, over Boston's final miles, Alberto could have backed off a notch and let Dick have his day. He could have saved himself.

But Alberto Salazar, of course, did not run marathons to save himself. He could no more have turned back from Boston, or away from Beardsley, than General Custer could have turned back from the Little Big Horn.

Now, in the winter of 1996 to '97, it was Beardsley's turn to watch the enemy warriors circling. He had to kick painkillers and methadone, face the press, appear in court, begin to heal the damage that he'd inflicted on his family, negotiate with his creditors, and squeeze in a day or two of work to begin to pay off his appalling debts. He had to perform all of these tasks out in the open, without opiates carousing in his blood and without the endlessly engrossing challenge of scoring pills to lend structure and meaning to his days.

Hour after hour, day after day, unrelenting reality jabbed Beardsley's stripped nervous system. Beyond the pain of drug withdrawal, there was the chronic pain in his back and knee that he'd incurred from his accidents. Pain ranged everywhere, in one form or another, and none of his old dodges were available to mitigate it. Denial, Beardsley's former ace in the hole, had been cut out of his deck. He couldn't even run or fish. For a month or two, there was the pallid solace of methadone, but eventually the time came to kick that, too. From a purely physical standpoint, this was the most difficult challenge of all. Over 18 harrowing days in February, Beardsley withdrew from methadone at the Fairview Riverside Recovery Center in Minneapolis. An almost equally taxing outpatient program followed.

Shooting toothache pains for 9 hours straight, but in his arms and legs not his teeth. He would've sliced them off if he had a knife sharp enough. Ten showers a night but he still itched everywhere. Each cell in his body itched, even his eyeballs. He shook so badly he had to crawl to breakfast, crawl to his chair in the group-therapy circle, which in its way was the biggest drag of all. When your turn came, you had to tell your story, which would be flayed bare by your fellow addicts—full-time, genetically predisposed junkies just like himself, who could sniff a grain of bullshit before it left your mouth. Sober, pitiless, stoked on coffee and cigarettes, they were led by Sue, head counselor and B.S. detector.

Sue and the other patients went easy on Beardsley at first, because he was a newbie. He was also a celebrity of sorts. His fall had made headlines, from the local TV news to the *New York Times*. His public ordeal earned him a modicum of sympathy, a margin of breathing room. But eventually the grace period expired and it was reality time, both barrels. Sue started the barrage. In a private therapy session, the counselor challenged Beardsley's relentless cheerfulness, insisting that it was phony, an act. Dick protested that he'd always been that way. He couldn't help it, couldn't change the way he was. Sue backed off, but that gave Beardsley a taste of things to come. There would be no charming this woman or his sister and brother addicts. He would have to turn around and face the shadow.

One night, outpatient now, near the butt-end of the endless Minnesota snowplow winter, Sue told him that it was his turn next week. Enough coddling, enough time to adjust. You are on, buddy. Tell us your story next time, and you better tell us the truth.

So on the day of the next group-therapy session, Dick blew off the whole afternoon and went to a mall in Fargo near the treatment center. He sat down in a coffee shop with a pen and a yellow legal pad and began to write. He started with the farm accident and then swung through the whole sorry 7-year chain of craving and pursuit and denial to the pivot of getting busted and on through to the present. Dick wrote and wrote, ripping at each page with his whole un-doped mind and heart, just the way he'd flung himself at the Boston Marathon 15 years earlier.

But as he wrote, it dawned on him that it was all connected. If he was really going to tell the truth, he would have to start much earlier. His entire life had been one long drive toward pills and toward this moment.

The northern lights dancing on below-zero morning runs Dad drunkenly screaming at Mom running down the gravel roads past barns in the summertime with George Ross eating ice-cold watermelon in the Ross's backyard Mary mumbling out from a dream in the hotel room at Boston past Heartbreak feeling nothing feeling everything Alberto behind him Alberto in front of him the motorcycles on Hereford Street finally stepping in the pothole. He could run again.

Ultramarathons consist of footraces longer than the official 26.2-mile marathon distance and fall into two broad categories, road races and trail races. The most famous trail ultra in the United States is the 100-Mile Western States Endurance Run, which follows a course along the spine of California's Sierra Nevada Mountains from Squaw Valley to Auburn. Requiring wilderness skills as much as running ability, trail ultras fell outside of Alberto Salazar's purview. But road ultras were another matter. The granddaddy of road ultras, the sport's equivalent of the Boston Marathon, was the Comrades Marathon, a 54-mile race held each May between the cities of Durban and Pietermaritzburg in the Natal province of South Africa.

Among the seismic shifts that Prozac catalyzed in a depressed person's psyche was an increased willingness to take risks. If he was going to enter the realm of ultramarathons, the resurgent Salazar reasoned, why not start at the top? So in the summer of 1993, Alberto resumed hard, focused training, aiming for the '94 Comrades.

Determined not to repeat past mistakes, he logged the bulk of his training on a treadmill in the basement of his Portland home. The treadmill, he felt, greatly reduced his chances of injury. The machine allowed him to progress in precisely calibrated increments, husband his newfound strength, and, most important, engage in focused prayer while he was working out. The rhythm of the belt and the whine of the motor, he discovered, formed an ideal backbeat for Hail Marys and Our Fathers. For the next 9 months, Alberto's usual ambient state consisted of churning 6 minutes a mile on the treadmill, while praying the rosary. He also lifted weights and performed other strength-training exercises; ultramarathoners, he had learned, required a margin of bulk to withstand the road's endless pounding.

Stay steady Hail Mary stay steady Our Father.

Comrades was held on a South African patriotic holiday at the end of May. Although this marked autumn in that latitude, the temperatures would still likely soar well into the 80s, with accompanying humidity. Yet again, Salazar had been called to a tradition-laced, hot-weather race. Comrades ran in opposite directions each year. On "down" years, the race started in Pietermaritzburg at an elevation of 2,400 feet, and headed east to the Indian Ocean coast at Durban, which lay at sea level. The next year would be "up," with the race heading in the ascending direction. Each direction offered its own kind of misery, wreaking havoc on a different part of the ultramarathoner's anatomy. The year 1994 happened to be an "up" year. Salazar cranked the treadmill to its steepest resistance, toiling toward a 54-mile footrace on the far side of the world.

In May 1994, accompanied by Molly, he took the back-to-back red-eye flight to Johannesburg. After 20 hours, he stepped out of the airplane into the shocking sunshine at Jan Smuts International Airport. A whiff of charcoal fires from the nearby Alexandra Township spiced the winey air. Fidel Castro's Cuba, the war-torn

Balkans, and now Nelson Mandela's South Africa: Salazar's destiny continued to lie in places of struggle and exile. As always, his presence drew considerable attention.

Newly emerged into the international community after decades of apartheid-related sanctions, South Africans were flattered and delighted that a famous American runner would travel so far to compete in a race intrinsic to their national identity. But at the same time, they were provincially defensive about Comrades. The South African media, citing the example of other proud foreign distance runners who had wrecked on the shoals of Comrades, discounted Salazar's chances of winning. A few sportswriters laid odds that he wouldn't even finish the race.

"That really focused me," Salazar said. "When people say I can't do something, it just makes me doubly determined. It was like when I ran the New York City Marathon for the first time. I was a rookie at the marathon. Nobody thought I could win or run a sub-2:10. It made my win all the sweeter, to prove my critics wrong."

To run effectively beyond a distance of 26 miles or a time span of around 2 hours, an athlete requires an outside source of carbohydrates that can be rapidly broken down into glycogen. How successfully a runner ingests fluids and calories during an ultramarathon usually decides the outcome of a race. At the starting line in Durban, Salazar taped several tubes of carbohydrate gel to his singlet and shorts. Race officials assured him that there would also be gel available at water stations throughout the course.

Alberto kissed Molly, who would ride along near him in a van. He found a group of runners who looked familiar and lined up next to them. The predawn air was soft and tropical, washed by a breeze off the ocean and tinged by something ancient and indefinable. He whispered a final pre-race prayer. A cannon boomed. Along with a field of 10,000 other runners, the great majority of whom would complete the withering 54-mile journey, Alberto set out for Pietermaritzburg.

Stay steady hit my splits stay steady hit my splits stay steady.

The African sun rose red and flaming out of the Indian Ocean behind him. On the pavement in front of him, his shadow took shape, reminiscent of the Boston Marathon—which at times seemed as if it happened yesterday, and at other times as if it had occurred in an earlier life. The highway climbed into the bush country of Zulu Natal. He ran past villages of circular thatched huts. Women walked among the villages, wearing brightly colored dresses, with stupendous loads balanced on their kerchiefed heads.

Stay steady hit my splits. 6:18 a mile, mile after mile.

The beep of his watch the chuff of his breath and every 5 minutes, remembering Boston, he lifted a water bottle to his lips. At the 20-mile mark, his 3-minute lead had grown to 5 minutes. But ahead on the press truck, the South African reporters guzzled beer and laughed scornfully at him.

At the 30-mile mark, Salazar finished the last of the gel tubes he'd packed with him. From this point on, he would have to take gel from the water stations. But despite the assurances of the race officials, there was no gel at the next water station, nor at any of the stations thereafter. He was exhausted. Molly was up ahead in the van, but there was no place for her to buy gel in the Natal outback, and his system wasn't conditioned to digest any other form of nourishment, not while he was running. There would be no more glycogen to power his muscles. Ten years ago, even 3 years ago,

Salazar would have exploded in anger. Now he realized there was nothing to do but quit the race or pray. The first option really was no option at all. Some things about him had not changed.

Alberto prayed out loud, in a full-throated voice. The spectators looked at him curiously, especially the Zulus. He did not know what faith they practiced, but they seemed to respect his prayers.

Hail Mary, full of grace, the Lord is with thee.

He stopped looking at Molly because every time he did so, he wanted to quit and crawl inside the cool darkness of the van and lie down beside her. *Hail Mary Our Father Hail Mary Our Father*, mile after mile.

Finally, the hill near Pietermaritzburg came into view. Polly Shorts Hill, Comrades' equivalent of Heartbreak Hill. The boys in the press truck had stopped laughing at him. Now they were rooting for him—the Cuban-American Prozac Catholic, running on empty, praying his way to Pietermaritzburg.

Groups of Zulu women stood by the road. As Salazar ran past, they ululated in tribute, their piercing, thrilling notes reminding him of the Wellesley women screaming at the halfway point at Boston, a mile away from where he had grown up.

After winning the 1994 Comrades in a time of 5 hours, 38 minutes, and 39 seconds, the equivalent of running two consecutive 2:44 marathons, Salazar flew back to the United States and continued training. He interpreted his triumph as a sign that God intended him to have a second career in ultramarathons. But just a few weeks after his return, while out on a training run, Salazar tore tendons in his ankle. He underwent surgery. The damage was clear and unequivocal. With nothing left to prove, Alberto Salazar retired from competitive distance running and began to coach.

20

Beardsley started to sprint. He put his head down and pumped his arms. He found another gear. He felt like angels were lifting him up. He made a hard right turn onto Hereford Street. He caught a glimpse of Salazar, like a glimpse of the Pope in a motorcade, 20 yards ahead, then put his head down again.

At the top of the hill, there was a hard left turn before the final straightaway. Salazar and the motorcycles made that turn, and the crowd at the finish line went wild, screaming in their hometown boy.

Beardsley had to weave his way through the motorcycles. The cops thought he was finished, but here he was back from the dead. They looked pie-faced and astonished as he pushed past them.

Salazar glanced back over his shoulder, also thinking that Beardsley was gone. But instead he was right there, on his shoulder, bearing down on him. Salazar's eyes grew as big as headlights. He turned to the finish line, the last hundred yards, with Beardsley in hell-hound pursuit.

Up in the TV booth above the finish line, Squires kept screaming, "Dickie! Dickie! Dickie!"

It was all clear to Salazar. There was nothing else to consider but the finish line up ahead, somewhere in that insane jumble of people and police barriers and motorcycles. The fact that he did not lose was as in-eluctable as a law of physics.

Hail Mary, full of grace. My God, Dick Beardsley was tough, but Alberto Salazar did not lose.

✦

Aboard the USS *John F. Kennedy* on patrol in the Indian Ocean, Lt. Ricardo Salazar had just fallen asleep when he was jarred awake by a sharp rap on his stateroom door. The orderly told him that he was to report to the captain, immediately. Ricardo dressed hurriedly and hustled up to the bridge, where the captain handed him a cablegram.

Ricardo glanced at the bottom of the message: *Yours truly, Sen. Edward F. Kennedy*. Ricardo knew this must have something to do with his father—Jose Salazar was constantly pressuring Kennedy about Cuba. His father must have arranged for the senator's office to send him a cablegram.

Then Ricardo scanned to the top of the cable: *"Your brother's bravery at today's Boston Marathon brought honor to all citizens of the Commonwealth of Massachusetts . . . "*

Only then did Ricardo recall that, in Massachusetts, on the other side of the world, it was Patriots' Day. Good God, Ricardo thought, had Alberto died?

He quickly read the entire letter. A tight smile spread across his face.

✦

On Tuesday morning, Dick took a half-hour jog, then greeted well-wishers in the Sheraton lobby, basking in his newfound fame. The newspapers ran adulatory headlines: "The Greatest Boston Marathon" and "An Epic Duel." Beardsley might have finished second, but he hadn't lost—the entire city reacted as if there had been two winners.

In the afternoon, New Balance executives chauffeured Mary and him around Boston in a limousine. They took him to corporate headquarters and, after the employees greeted him with a standing ovation, wrote him a generous new multiyear contract. Agents from all the major road races were after him to run, or even to simply make an appearance, promising fees he only might have dreamed of 48 hours earlier. Officials from Grandma's Marathon in Duluth were especially insistent, virtually begging him to return to their race to defend his 1981 title. But Grandma's would be run in June, just 7 weeks after Boston. There was no way Dick could recover that fast. Or was there?

Beardsley traveled to Alaska to think it over. He had previously committed to running a 10-K road race in Anchorage. The race directors there assured him his trip would be little more than a vacation—just come up and take it easy, jog through the 10-K, meet people, shake hands. But it wasn't in Dick's nature to take it easy, at least not during a road race. And once he got to Alaska, it seemed like every runner in the state wanted to take their best shot at the man who had nearly conquered Alberto Salazar. Beardsley wasn't about to back down to them. He ran the 10-K flat out and did the same at several other road races around Anchorage.

Then he returned to Minnesota and, despite the pleading of Squires, Mary, and others, said yes to Grandma's. The people there had been so good to him, and Grandma's was his home state's showcase marathon, and his 2:09 win there last year had put him on the map . . . he simply couldn't say no. In June, Dick traveled to Duluth and, running on a badly frayed Achilles tendon, slogged through to a 2:14:49 victory that sealed his eventual doom as a professional athlete. In October, he showed up for the New York City Marathon, but his eagerly anticipated rematch with Salazar turned into an anticlimactic flop. Beardsley finished 30th in 2:18:12.

That winter, he underwent the first in a series of Achilles tendon surgeries that kept him out of the 1984 Olympic marathon trials. Through the next few years, he launched repeated comeback attempts, logging a few decent marathons, but nothing approaching the transcendence of the '82 Boston. After finishing a deflating 45th in the 1988 Olympic trials, Dick Beardsley retired from professional competition. With the '82 Boston to look back on, he had surprisingly little trouble letting go.

The café at Nike's Mia Hamm Building is just about deserted. Alberto Salazar's quick lunch break has turned into a 3-hour retrospective of his life and career—just a few minutes more than it once took him to run a marathon.

Finally, Salazar rises from the table. In the lobby, before riding the elevator up to his office, he says, "At the time of the Boston Marathon, I didn't know Dick very well. And to be honest, for a long time afterward, I sort of resented him. Well, that passed, like a lot of my stuff passed." He gives a terse shake of his head.

"Then in 2002, the Boston Marathon brought us back for the

20th anniversary of our race. We got to know each other. Now, among all the guys I ran with or against, Dick might be the one I feel closest to. I'll pick up the phone every few months and give him a call. I think he and I have a special bond. All that he's gone through . . . I'm not saying I can understand it, but maybe I can come close.

"We both give a lot of talks, to all kinds of groups, all over the country," Salazar continues. "Sooner or later, someone always asks about the '82 Boston. I don't mind—I like talking about it, and so does Dick. That's because we never discuss the race in terms of running a 2:08 or beating the other guy. It took us both a long, long time, but we finally realized that that's not what the marathon is really about. It's not what it's about at all."

❂

"After the race, people came up to me and said, 'Gosh Dick, if you hadn't had to fight through all those police motorcycles, you might have won,'" Beardsley recalls for his audience at the Royal Victoria Marathon. "But I don't look at it that way. I ran the race of my life, 2:08:53. Alberto happened to run 2 seconds faster. All I know for certain is that I left everything I had out on that course. I didn't give an inch. Neither did Alberto. The way I look at it, there were two winners that day."

The crowd erupts in applause. Beardsley lets the cheers wash over him for a moment, then holds his hands up for quiet.

"Tomorrow, at your marathon, you're going to give it your all," he tells the crowd. "When it's over, you can look back on a job well done. You'll be able to relax. You'll be finished.

"Well, the race that I'm running now, I can never relax, never be finished," Beardsley goes on. "The day I say that I've got my addiction beat, I'll be in greater danger than when my leg got caught in that power takeoff. I can't let that day come. I just celebrated my seventh year of sobriety. Those have been the 7 hardest years of my life. They have also been the 7 best years. Every morning, I feel like I'm getting up to run the Boston Marathon all over again."

EPILOGUE

For several years, Dick Beardsley had been trying to bring Alberto Salazar to his half-marathon in Detroit Lakes, and in September 2003 he finally succeeded. That month was extremely busy for Salazar, both as a coach and as a parent. Marking the start of the competitive cross-country season, early September formed a critical period for Galen Rupp and the other kids on Salazar's Central Catholic High School team. Dan Browne and the Oregon Project runners, meanwhile, were wrapping up the summer track season and looking ahead to fall marathons. Alberto's sons, Alex and Tony, were respectively immersed in college soccer and football. Maria, Alberto's youngest child, conceived after the Salazars' first pilgrimage to Medjugorje and named for the Holy Mother, was starting seventh grade.

Despite these pressures and obligations, Alberto agreed to travel to Minnesota. He wanted to help Dick, and realized that future Septembers would likely be just as hectic as this one. He also believed that there was more virtue in sacrificing to help a friend than in doing so at one's own convenience. In the 21 years since his Boston Marathon victory, much had changed about Alberto Salazar, but not his ironclad sense of propriety and duty.

So on the Friday after Labor Day, Alberto boarded a plane in Portland, headed for Fargo. As far as he could recall, it would be his second time in North Dakota. He wouldn't be in the state for long. Representatives from the race would pick him up at the airport and then drive 45 minutes to Detroit Lakes in Minnesota. His first stop would be the local high school, where he would meet Beardsley and visit with a group of teenage runners. That evening, Salazar would give a brief talk at the pre-race pasta dinner. The next morning, he would shake a few hands, say a few more words, then run the half-marathon. Less than 24 hours after arriving in Detroit Lakes, Alberto would be heading back to Fargo and his flight home.

The brief but intense visit was typical of many Salazar made at road races around the country. Even relatively minor, out-of-the-way events now included an expo with celebrity speakers, corporate marketing, and a Web site. Everything about the sport and business of distance running had improved exponentially over the last 21 years—everything, that is, but the marathon performances of native-bred American men. As he settled into his seat for the 3-hour flight, Alberto fingered his rosary beads. He calculated that he'd be able to work through the rosary several times during the trip out. People always complained that there was no time to pray, but Salazar, among the busiest of men, found plenty of time: the fluid, spectral, netherworld moments waiting to fall asleep at night; the stark, pit-of-the-night hours when sleep wouldn't come; commuting on the freeway to the Nike campus in Beaverton; sitting on airplanes. So many empty hours could be redeemed, he maintained, if people only set their minds to the task, if they opened themselves toward grace.

But people tended to be lazy. When he was younger, Alberto couldn't understand why other runners refused to work and sacrifice to the extent that he did. Now, as a coach, he realized that most athletes—including many of the most talented—simply lacked the drive, the capacity to endure pain, that Salazar had been blessed and cursed with. By the same token, people manufactured every reason imaginable not to pray and observe the sacraments. Such sloth once irked Alberto, but he had grown more forgiving of others' weaknesses. Most people, he had learned, simply lacked his hunger and capacity for prayer. For this reason, Salazar made a point of leading his Central Catholic runners in prayer—publicly, out loud, with head bowed and eyes closed—before each workout and race. It was his duty to set an example, show the kids that faith was not just a quaint anachronism but a living force. He knew that some people ridiculed him for it. They laughed behind his back, thought that he was a fool or worse—a hypocrite, a show-off, a phony.

But just as Alberto had trained the way he saw fit in his previous lifetime, he prayed as he saw fit in this one. This weekend in Minnesota presented another chance to witness. At times, he wondered if he should have been a priest. Other times, he thought that if he hadn't been an athlete, he almost certainly would have gone into the military, like his two brothers.

As his plane sailed east over Idaho, Montana, and the Dakotas, Alberto tried to relax, but couldn't escape a mild stirring of anxiety. Instead of merely watching tomorrow's race, he had committed to running the half-marathon. No one would expect him to compete seriously, of course, but they would still expect him to . . . well, be Alberto Salazar. He hadn't run that far in more than a year. You couldn't fake your way through 13.1 miles. The people would see him struggle. Every step Alberto ever ran had been under pressure. During the brief years of his prime, he'd been able to mask the warping that pressure exacted. But now that he was a balding, middle-aged man with stiff legs, just trying to get through a race, he could no longer hide the cost of each step. Even in Detroit Lakes, Minnesota, running formed a challenge—a kind of moral predicament—for Alberto Salazar.

The plane descended into Fargo. Alberto gazed down at the

green country. Despite his hard-won serenity and the intensely social nature of his job, a quality of separateness still emanated from Salazar. He would never become a natural extrovert like Dick Beardsley. Being too much with others drained him rather than charged him. He hadn't taken Prozac since 1997. Perhaps he occasionally wished that a small, manufactured lift were still an option. Salazar closed his eyes and touched his rosary beads. It would all be over in 24 hours.

As always, Alberto looked terrific. Well into his forties, Salazar had the same glow that he had displayed the first time Beardsley saw him, 25 years ago in New York City, cutting around Manhattan in that black leather jacket. Salazar seemed cut from a different cloth than most other distance runners. Dick could never imagine Alberto flailing around in high school the way he had. Beardsley had been so desperate to impress girls by winning a varsity letter that he tried out for football his junior year. The coach advised the 110-pound boy against it. When he persisted, the coach designated him the cow in a game of tackle-the-cow. Dick got the football, the bulls gang-tackled him, and he fled football for cross-country. That sport nearly killed him, too. For his first practice, he showed up in a pair of basketball sneakers, knee socks, and a pair of his father's Bermuda shorts. The coach ordered the team out on a 2-mile run. Beardsley took off at a dead sprint and after a quarter mile had to lie down.

That story now formed one of Dick's most popular set pieces during his talks. In fact, at bottom, he was just as much a geek now as he was as a 16-year-old. He still wore goofy hats, still loved cows, still cried at sad stories, and still told corny jokes. But most runners could relate. The sport induced a certain humility. It wasn't like you were throwing a ball around out there. You were constantly struggling against the distance and against yourself. There was never a guarantee that you'd prevail. The marathon especially was such a long, hard way to go. Anything could happen over 26.2 miles. The sport did not lend itself to pride or poses.

Alberto's pride, however, had never been a pose. There had never been anything phony or affected about his air of self-confidence. Rather than being an awkward loner, he naturally aligned with elite outfits such as the Greater Boston Track Club, the University of Oregon, and Nike. Even after 25 years, after all that they had been through, separately and together—after both men had very publicly exposed their feet of clay—Beardsley remained a little in awe of Salazar.

Greeting the kids at Detroit Lakes High School, Alberto wore a blue T-shirt and a white Nike cap. A small Nike swoosh tattoo was visible on his bicep, beneath the sleeve of the shirt. The clothes attractively set off his deep tan and white smile. He had put on a few pounds, which he carried gracefully on his big frame. All the girls and women twittered around Alberto. Such a glamorous hunk rarely appeared in Detroit Lakes. As always when he was nervous (or relaxed, or excited, or even down in the dumps), Beardsley started to chatter.

"Well, Al, great to see ya. You wouldn't believe the response we got when people found out you were coming. So here's the program—after we finish here at the school we'll go into town and I'll show you around if you want, or take you straight to your motel. I'm afraid we don't have a lot of fancy places in Detroit Lakes, but I think you'll be comfortable at the Best Western. I got you a room in the rear building away from the highway and railroad tracks. Those freight trains go by all night long but pretty soon you don't even hear them anymore. Yeah, sure, I'll take you to the motel, you must be shot . . . "

Alberto just smiled through all of Dick's yammering. Salazar seemed relaxed, focused, and well-rested, even after the long flight. The tension had drained from his face. Back in the old days, Alberto's face had always been tight, dark, and clouded. Look at that photo of Alberto and Dick right after Boston, when they stood together on the victory platform. You'd think Al would be ecstatic, or at least relieved, but instead he looked like he still carried the weight of the world. Now, however, Al's eyes were clear and calm. You didn't feel like he was going to jump down your throat if you said the wrong thing.

People don't usually change that much, Beardsley reflected. At bottom, for instance, he hadn't changed. He had been turned inside out. He had trashed everything that had been granted him. He had used and abused the people he loved and done his level best to destroy himself. (Why hadn't he died? Why was he still around?) He had jumped up and down to show the world that he wasn't the man that he appeared to be. Yes, Dick had been through just about everything possible in the last 20 years, but he hadn't really changed. He was the same man that he'd always been. The same farm boy, the same optimist, the same fool. Even moving through the 12-step program—a transformation package, a psychic boot camp—had only brought him back to his true self. Sometimes Dick thought that a person's inability to change was one of the most depressing facts of life. Other times, he thought that it was one of the most hopeful.

Whatever, the point was that Alberto Salazar *had* changed. He seemed to be a different man than the one who had refused to mention Dick's name before the '82 Boston. He gave off different waves. Watching Alberto work so easily and unaffectedly with the high school kids, Dick felt the same way he had 21 years earlier, running beside Alberto on the approach to Heartbreak. This is so cool, he thought, but also the slightest bit unnerving.

When they finished at the high school, Salazar climbed into Beardsley's truck. As they drove away, Alberto started talking about Galen Rupp. A gleam rose in his eye. It was as if Dan Browne and the Oregon Project and the Altitude House (the Nike-developed runners' residence in Portland where pressurized rooms simulated conditions of 10,000 feet elevation) and all the rest were what he did to pay the rent, but what Alberto did on his own time, to feed his heart, was tend to Galen.

Beardsley regularly surfed the running Web sites, and he still subscribed to the running magazines. He had heard that the kid was something special. Now, listening to Alberto rave about him, Dick knew that Rupp was the real goods. Al explained that Galen had started out as a soccer player at Central Catholic, the Portland high school where Alberto coached. The soccer coach told Al that Galen never got tired when he played and ought to give cross-country a shot. Salazar gave him a tryout, and the boy had never looked back. Galen was tough, competitive, strong, fast, smart, and charismatic. He had that X factor that only the special ones—Prefontaine, Salazar—possessed. Dick had seen some photos. Galen was a beautiful kid to look at, on the run and otherwise. More important, he could handle the pain. Alberto made it crystal clear to the boy how hard he and Beardsley and other runners had pushed themselves 25 years ago, and the kid still signed on.

Now, Alberto was molding him. Dick could understand why Alberto was so excited. Imagine having the chance to go back and live your life over again—in Salazar's case, get struck by lightning all over again. It was like a great painter coming back at the end of his career and teaching a young artist who seemed every bit the genius as his mentor. Al was working on Galen with the finest materials imaginable. He knew every turn in the road where the boy could go wrong. What an opportunity, Dick thought. What a responsibility. What would happen if Alberto blew it again?

They drove into Detroit Lakes' modest downtown. The home of Dick Beardsley fishing guide service, the Dick Beardsley fishing show on local cable TV, Dick Beardsley motivational speaking, Dick Beardsley running camp, Mary Beardsley house cleaning. He couldn't imagine living anywhere else. It was small potatoes compared to Alberto's operation, but every day, Dick was thankful for it. In his late forties, he'd struck a happy, steady balance in his life.

Everybody knew him here. He didn't have anything to hide. Not that he would try to hide anything anyway. Dick had had his fill of concealment. Five years of hiding had nearly destroyed him. Now everything was out in the open, and he never felt happier. His guide business was booming. Regular customers kept him going, reserving days on the lake a year in advance. He was especially pleased by the fact that most of his clients didn't know anything about his background—running or drugs. They just knew Beardsley as a man they could trust with their lives, who was great company out on a lake, so much fun, that it didn't matter whether they caught any fish or not. In fact, business was so robust that he had to divert some clients to other guides. Those guys could get a little bit jealous, sure. Detroit Lakes wasn't perfect. But the town had stood behind him during his troubles.

Back in that black December of 1995, Beardsley had been so frightened and depressed that he hadn't wanted to go out of the house. But when he finally ventured out to the bait shop, the guys had rallied around him. People came up to him on the street—some of the town's leading citizens—and shook his hand and admitted to him that they had been through something similar. Drinking, pills, every kind of drug you could imagine. It was all right here in Detroit Lakes. People you wouldn't expect in a million years. Of course, no one would've expected Dick in a million years either.

"Hey, I'll show you around a little bit," he told Alberto. Dick loved to cruise around in his pickup. He would have kept a gun rack in the cab were it not for the fact that he still had that felony on his record and, for another few years, couldn't legally possess a firearm in Minnesota.

He drove down the six-block-long commercial strip, then swung onto Highway 10 by the train tracks and motel, heading for the lake. Dick explained to Alberto that tomorrow's race would make two loops around the lake—it was a good flat, scenic course. Alberto remarked that the lake looked beautiful in the late summer sunshine.

"September is the best time of year up here," Beardsley agreed. "But you ought to come back in January. The lake looks a little different then."

On a January morning in the pit of the northwoods winter when the arctic cold rolls down from the polar heart of Canada and the temperature dips to 40 below zero and the lake freezes so deep and solid that you can drive your rig over it without a thought when you set up your fishing hut. And in the blackest and coldest part of the day, the silent 4:00 and 5:00 a.m. hour when the stars burn down cold fire, that is when Dick still rose from his warm bed to run his 6-mile loop around the lake. The wind searing his cheeks through the woolen mask and his breath billowing out in great locomotive chuffs. The air glittering crystalline and his blood beating hot and on certain snowless mornings the

*northern lights putting on such a show for Dick alone that his
knees nearly buckled. That is then when he prayed in his fashion,
because just being out there, running, was prayer enough.*

Alberto seemed happy to take in the sights, but Dick sensed that he
was humoring him more than truly enjoying himself. Dick, by contrast, loved visiting new places. That was one of the things he liked
best about his athletic career. The idea that someone in a far-off
city—London, New York, Boston—would invite him to travel to
their town and run their race. And then to get paid for all that . . .
well, what more could Dick say about it? Over the last few years,
as his seemingly intractable injuries healed, he had gradually
worked back into the sport, going from jogging a few miles to running the lake at dawn three times a week to running daily. Then,
what the heck, cruising through one of the 10-Ks that had invited
him to speak. And hey, it didn't feel so bad, so why not run the first
half of the next marathon he spoke at? Completely unofficially, of
course, just for fun? Those 13 miles went like a dream. When he
hit the halfway point, he just kept going. He finished the whole
26.2 miles. He felt so good afterward that he did the next
marathon a little faster, really running this time. Pretty soon he was
training 50 or 60 miles a week, and his marathon time had dipped
into the 2:40s.

Greg Meyer, whose 1983 Boston Marathon victory had been
the most recent win in a major marathon by a native-bred
American man, once warned Beardsley that he wouldn't want to
run when he got older because he would be so much slower than
in his glory days. But Dick had never felt that way. He loved
pushing himself; he loved improving, no matter at what speed. In
fact, if some shoe company came along and said, Dick, we'll pay
you a monthly salary for the next few years and all you have to do

is train and see how fast you can make your old body move . . . well, he'd take it in a heartbeat.

But Beardsley got the impression that Alberto felt differently—about traveling and about running itself. Alberto seemed relieved to be done with running—at least, done with it personally.

"So, Al, if it's okay with you, I'd like to tape a half-hour interview with you for the local cable TV station," he said to his guest in the truck. "The studio is right here on the main street in town. Great people. They produce my fishing show. Every week during the summer, I visit a different lake in the area and talk about some aspect of the sport. People seem to like it. In fact, I've been talking to the PBS affiliate in Fargo about picking up the show. That would mean a much bigger audience. So, anyway, it'll just take a half an hour, we can do it anytime, now let's go get you settled in the motel . . . "

But in a crisp, almost military fashion, Alberto said no, Dick, let's do it now—get it done, crossed off the list, don't let it linger. So Beardsley swung his pickup around on the sunny main street, parked, waved to everybody passing by, proudly introducing his famous guest. He led Alberto into the small storefront studio, refreshingly cool and dark after the hot glare outside. The producer miked up Alberto and situated him against a dark blue backdrop, which contrasted nicely with Alberto's white ball cap, deeply tanned face, and white teeth. Dick took a seat facing him, off-camera, and fired away.

"Alberto, it's great to have you."

"It's great to be here, Dick," Alberto said with a warm smile.

"Some people are gonna think we're racing against each other like another duel in the sun 21 years later."

"I'm already conceding," Salazar said, with another gracious smile. "I'll be behind you, I know that for sure. My goal is just to complete the distance. This will be the farthest I've run in more than a year."

Beardsley asked about Salazar's world-record marathon at New York City. "I did what I aimed to do in that race," Alberto said. "That's about the best you can expect out of life. Everything went perfectly during that run. It was a once-in-a-lifetime experience."

Finally, Dick arrived at the subject of the '82 Boston Marathon, beginning with Salazar's 10,000-meter race against Henry Rono at Hayward Field the week before. Time had scoured away the seamy, surreal edge. So now Rono was not a drunken reprobate but only a supremely tough and gifted runner who, despite being 10 to 15 pounds overweight, prevailed in the race. "Which shows you what a great runner Henry was," Alberto said, still smiling.

For a moment it was so quiet that they could hear the hum of the air conditioner. The artfully projected light of the studio cast no shadows. Beardsley framed his next question carefully. "Al, coming home to run the Boston Marathon, was there a lot of pressure on you?"

For a moment it was as if the sun went behind a cloud. "Most of the pressure I ever felt was self-imposed," Alberto said. "I put a lot of pressure on myself. More than I should have, more than was healthy. When I didn't run well, I didn't throw tantrums, but inside I was very mad at myself. I would be hard on myself for weeks or even months afterward. When a marathon was over, it was like a huge weight had lifted off my shoulders. I think that the best moment of a marathon was just afterward, soaking in the tub, with no more people around, no more expectations."

After another moment's pause, Dick said, "Al, I can't thank you enough for pushing me all the way up to the end."

Salazar nodded. "I look at that marathon as the epitome of what running is all about," he said. "There hasn't been a Boston

Marathon since where the two favorites ran together all the way from Hopkinton, doing everything possible to beat each other, neither one giving an inch. I think it was the greatest American distance race."

"I agree," Beardsley said.

The next morning, the two men went out into the sunshine to meet the people of Detroit Lakes and run the half-marathon. During the time they spent together, they did not speak of their troubles—of Salazar's depression or of Beardsley's addiction. Neither one pointed out the irony that while drugs nearly destroyed Dick, they helped save Alberto. Neither mentioned the searing demarcation that the 1982 Boston Marathon had etched in their lives. There was no need. They were with the only other person in the world who understood the true cost of that race.

At the starting line, the citizen-runners eagerly snapped photos of the two champions. Each man held the microphone and said a brief word. Then the gun sounded and they set out running, side by side. Beardsley moved fluidly and Salazar stiffly. They ran into the morning sun, so that their shadows fell behind them.

PHOTO CREDITS

INDEX

Boldface references indicate photographs.